Photograph taken by author, 2025. Edited via Canva.

"We are not human beings having a spiritual experience. We are spiritual beings having a human experience." – Anonymous, but often attributed to Pierre Teilhard de Chardin

Being Guided: Lessons from Your Inner Beloved

Copyright © 2025 by Scott D. Smith

All rights reserved. No part of this book may be reproduced, distributed, or transmitted in any form or by any means, including photocopying, recording, or other electronic or mechanical methods, without the prior written permission of the author, except as permitted by U.S. copyright law.

The views and opinions expressed in this book are those of the author and do not necessarily reflect the official policy or position of any other individual or entity.

Final Edition, January, 2026
Version 1.0

Printed in the United States of America

ISBN 979-8-9931540-0-8 (EPUB)
ISBN 979-8-9931540-1-5 (PDF)
ISBN 979-8-9931540-2-2 (Hardback)
ISBN 979-8-9931540-3-9 (Paperback)

This copyright applies to both printed and digital editions of this work.

The publisher nor the author is giving professional advice or services to the reader. The ideas, procedures, and suggestions herein are not intended to substitute for consulting with your therapist or physician. All matters regarding your health require medical supervision. Neither the author nor the publisher is liable or responsible for any loss or damage allegedly arising from any information or suggestions in this book.

The front cover was a photograph taken by the author, a design created using Canva.

Photograph of the labyrinth at St. James the Apostle Episcopal Church, Tempe, Arizona: © 2023 Scott Hensley. Used with permission.

The image of the dream wheel in chapter 3 was created by the author using Canva.

The photograph in chapter 3 was taken by the author in 2025.

The image of the Kintsugi soul cup in chapter 4: photo by [Matt Perkins](.) on [Unsplash](.) (free under Unsplash License).

Testimonials

"Personally I do appreciate your book.. the inner beloved experience is essential in the path of individuation." Marie-Laure Colonna, Jungian psychoanalyst, author, and supervising member of the IAAP.

"I really, really like this [getting stuck subsection]. I've been using it all week. Hope you don't mind. But I paraphrased it about why clients get stuck because they aren't following their inner voice, guide, or as Campbell said their 'bliss'." – Dana Scott, Licensed Master Social Worker (LMSW).

"Lovely that you've done this. Both our own Red books in different formats." – R. A Falconer, author of "Soul Songs Anthology."

"When I finished this chapter [one], I sat in silence for a moment. It didn't feel like I'd just read a piece of writing. It felt like I'd been in a quiet room with someone speaking softly about something sacred. There's warmth here, and a strange comfort that comes from knowing someone else has also looked inward and found both light and shadow there." – Marc Frecky, digital content professional and beta reader.

Dedication

To my wife, Lynette, the love of my life. Without you, I would have accomplished nothing of note.

To Maxwell, my inner beloved. You guided my hand in writing this book. I am sorry that I could not use you as the 'pen name' for this book.

Acknowledgements

To Claudio, who gifted me with his nuanced understanding of Tor's user illusion.

To Llewellyn Vaugh-Lee, author of *Bond with The Beloved,* who opened my eyes to this deep, inner relationship I've always had.

To Lynette, who brought much-needed editorial wisdom to the text.

To Marc and Amanda, who encouraged me to warm up the text and keep it focused on the inner beloved. To Amanda, again, for encouraging me not to write advice based on personality tests.

To Stan, who realized that I had written the text for the Preface without realizing it. It's much better organized now! Thanks also for suggesting the topic of my next book.

To Svein, who wisely warned me not to screw with it too much. I listened as best I could, my friend. Thanks also for keeping the Finding Your Calling chapter focused on the inner beloved. I guess I will need to take Stan's advice and write a Management book next! To Svein again, for dissuading me from writing a chapter based on personality tests.

Contents

Forward by Dana Scott, LMSW 12
Preface 13
    What Is This Book About? 13
    Two Brains, One Soul 15
    What Is Our Inner Beloved? 18
    The Dangers of Perfectionism 20
    References 23
1 Understanding Your Inner Beloved **27**
    Saying a Prayer to Your Inner Self 28
    The Parable of the Overflowing Cup 28
    A Lesson: What Am I Carrying? 30
    Getting Unstuck 32
    A Lesson: Helping You Get Unstuck 36
    References 39
2 Making the Invitation **41**
    A Lesson: Helping You to Relax 42
    A Lesson: Making an Invitation to Your Inner Beloved 43
    A Lesson: Meeting Your Inner Beloved 43
    Your Inner Beloved Is a Companion 45
    References 48
3 Dreaming a Conversation **49**
    The Dream of the Nun That Changed into an Elephant 50
    Being Persistent 57
    Doubting Messages About the Future 57
    What If You Can't Remember Your Dreams? 59
    References 60
4 Being Guided by Your Imagination **61**
    Taking Cautions Before You Proceed 62
    Talking to Your Inner Self 64

    A Lesson: Having an Inner Conversation............................ 65
    Using Powerful Emotions to Heal You................................ 66
    Performing a Healing Ritual.. 68
    What If an Inner Image Is Negative?..................................... 70
    What If My Inner Beloved Is Silent or Unnoticed?............. 74
    References.. 87

5 Finding Your Inner Path..93
    Finding Creativity Versus Forcing It......................................94
    Realizing the Source and Purpose of Your Inner Path......... 95
    A Lesson: Showing Me My Path.. 96
    Understanding the Spiritual Meaning of an Inner Path........98
    Distinguishing Inner Wealth Versus Ego Wealth................. 99
    A Lesson: What Is the Currency of Your Soul?................. 100
    Finding Inner Wealth..102
    Walking the Labyrinth with Your Soul............................... 103
    References.. 107

6 Finding Your Calling... 109
    A Lesson: Whose Life Are You Living?............................. 109
    Lending Your Abilities to Your Work and Your Talents to Your Soul..112
    Realizing Creativity Is Not All-Or-Nothing........................113
    Bringing Soul into the Workplace.. 115
    Practicing Servant Leadership..116
    Finding a Soulful Vocation...118
    Walking Joyfully Through the Fire..................................... 120
    References.. 122

7 Finding Good Relationships..125
    A Lesson: Being a Friend to Yourself................................. 126
    Knowing Yourself Through Others...................................... 128
    Finding Relationships Vs. Seeking Them........................... 130
    Finding Mystical Companionship.. 131
    Caring For Your Soul.. 133

Creating (Curating) Yourself..135
Forgiving Yourself and Others...136
A Lesson: Forgiving..137
Worrying Less and Living More..141
A Lesson: Worrying Less and Living More...................................142
Healing Family Relationships..145
Handling Community Relationships..146
Understanding That the End Is a New Beginning...........................148
A Letter to Arline from Rich..149
References...150

8 Being Creative and Playful..153
A Lesson: Inviting Playfulness...154
Following the Playful Path to Your Unconscious............................155
Staying Grounded in Your Soul..156
Understanding Why Art Matters..157
Avoiding Traps of Being an Artist..158
Doing Ordinary Artsy Things..159
Innovating: A Multidisciplinary Approach.....................................161
Using Creativity in Therapy...162
References...165

9 Practicing Spirituality..169
Saying a Prayer to Your Inner Beloved...169
Distinguishing Spirituality from Religion......................................171
Making Spirituality Your Religion...172
Having a Profound Experience Will Heal You...............................174
Encountering the Self..175
Facing the Soul Instead of Worshiping False Gods........................177
Focusing on Your Own Sacred Conversations...............................178
Being in Service to Others...179
Achieving Self-Awareness...182
References..185

A Using Mindfulness Techniques..191

    A Lesson: Simple Box Breathing..................................191
    A Lesson: Simple Meditation......................................193
    A Lesson: Basic Active Imagination............................194
    A Lesson: The Observer/Conductor Dialogue...............196
    Using Tips and Tricks for Inner Dialogue......................198
    References...200

B Using Oracles...201
    A Lesson: Using the I Ching.......................................202
    How Alana Uses the I Ching......................................203
    Using Tarot for Self-Reflection....................................204
    A Lesson: Using Tarot.. 205
    References...207

C Communing With Your Inner Beloved......................209

D Using Miscellaneous Lessons..................................211
    A Lesson: A Script for Safety and Protection...............211
    A Lesson: A Dialogue Between Your Thinking and Feeling Parts..214
    A Lesson: Gardening and Being in Nature.................. 215
    A Lesson: 5-4-3-2-1 Sensory Grounding......................217
    A Lesson: Body Mindfulness......................................218
    References...220

E Glossary..221
    Active Imagination..221
    Anima / Animus..221
    Archetypes..222
    Box Breathing.. 222
    Cognitive-Behavioral Therapy (CBT)........................... 223
    Collective Unconscious...223
    Dream Wheel & Spokes Method................................ 224
    Ego... 224
    Embodiment / Somatic practices.................................224
    Individuation or Shadow Integration............................ 225

Inner Beloved / Guide.. 225
Inner Child (puer aeternus).. 225
Inner Narrative / Inner Mythology.............................226
Integration / Shadow Integration................................226
Internal Family Systems (IFS)................................... 227
Journaling / Self-talk..227
Jungian Analytical Psychology...................................228
Labyrinth..228
Mandala..228
Magical Other..228
MBTI (Myers-Briggs Type Indicator).........................229
Narrative or Storytelling Therapy................................229
Numinous...229
Objective Observer..230
Parts Dialogue / Parts Work.. 230
Persona..230
Prayer.. 231
Projections / Withdrawing Projections........................231
Psychic Phenomenon.. 231
Puer aeternus / Eternal Child.......................................232
Red book... 232
Ritual / Healing Ritual / Symbolic Ritual................... 233
Self versus self.. 233
Servant Leadership..233
Shadow / Shadow Complex / Shadow Integration.............233
Soul / Soul Guide / Inner Beloved.............................. 234
Spiritual Bypassing... 234
Transcendent Function..235
Transference and Countertransference........................235
Unconscious (personal and collective)........................236
Witnessing (thoughts)... 236
References...237

Forward by Dana Scott, LMSW

I have known Scott for over a decade, and in that time I've witnessed both his depth of thought and his deep compassion for the human journey. *Being Guided: Lessons From Your Inner Beloved* is a reflection of that and an exploration of the psyche that is both profoundly Jungian and deeply personal.

Scott approaches the inner world with the curiosity of a scholar and the tenderness of a seeker. His work reminds us that the path toward wholeness is not one of perfection, but of integration–of coming to know and embrace all that we are.

Reading this feels like sitting across from an old friend who sees beyond words, someone who gently invites you to listen for the quiet voice of the soul. Scott's insights will challenge you, comfort you, maybe make you mad! But that's what Jungians do, especially with shadow work. Ultimately, though, his book is a call to you toward a deeper love of your own becoming.

It is an honor to know Scott and to witness the unfolding of his book. I believe it will touch the hearts of all who are willing to journey inward and encounter their own beloved within.

Your Friend,

Dana Scott

Preface

"Together the patient and I address ourselves to the 2,000,000-year-old man that is in all of us. In the last analysis, most of our difficulties come from losing contact with our instincts, with the age-old unforgotten wisdom stored up in us."
— C. G. Jung (1936)

What Is This Book About?

The purpose of this book is personal transformation: to re-establish a relationship with your imaginary friend from childhood. Allow me to introduce you to your inner beloved, the unconscious companion in your mind. This book will focus on the conversation that your *ego** has with your inner beloved. The guidance you receive via inner conversations provides important balance and wisdom throughout your life (Jung, 1969; Vaughan-Lee, 1993). **Terms in italic are defined in the glossary*

To me, the inner beloved is a product of what neurobiologists call ancient evolutionary brain structures. We know this ancient brain from early life, when we play, acquire language, and interact with our imaginary friend as we grow up (MacLean, 1990).

As we mature, the cerebral cortex develops dominance, giving us the gifts of logic and ordered thinking. This transition often creates problems for adolescents, who begin to overthink, experience anxiety, and become prone to loss of meaning, depression, and obsessive thoughts (Casey, Jones, & Hare, 2008). Our ancestors addressed these challenges with rites and rituals of initiation, designed to integrate the ancient brain with the modern brain into a lifetime partnership (van Gennep, 1960; Eliade, 1958). Neither the ego nor the inner beloved should be in charge of you; instead, the two must work together, enabling the individual to thrive in a creative romance of art and logic. This inner relationship with the self has defined humanity for hundreds of thousands of years (Jung, 1969).

Rituals that integrate mind and *soul* persist, but the rapid pace of technological change has sidelined them. Today, most people experience only minimal initiation into adulthood: getting a driver's license, graduating from school, getting married, and a few others. As a result, most people have lost touch with their inner beloved. People often live stressed and unhappy lives because their egos are isolated, without inner guidance, in a bewildering world that changes chaotically (Moore, 1992; Jung, 1969).

However, you do not have to be alone on this journey through life.

About a century ago, as people sought help for their struggles with a hyper-rationalist world, various schools of psychotherapy emerged to assist suffering clients in integrating the wisdom of their ancient brain with the rational modern brain. This book draws on the writings of thinkers and therapists who have developed methods to help clients make a partnership with their inner beloved. In this way, they can reintroduce themselves to their inner beloved and enter it into a partnership with their adult ego. This partnership, which should last a lifetime, helps people live happier, more productive lives. This partnership with the inner self makes people less susceptible to the modern afflictions of runaway rationality (Stein, 1998; Singer, 1994).

For those without a diagnosed serious mental illness or disability, these techniques are used to integrate a client's personal unconscious, or shadow, in a process Jung (1968c) called *individuation*.

Two Brains, One Soul

Our two brains (ancient and modern) form a partnership of wisdom and cleverness (MacLean, 1990). When the modern brain gets out of balance with the ancient brain, we get symptoms of neurosis, which in modern terms manifest as depression, anxiety, and addiction (MacLean, 1990; Price & Friston, 2019). Humans for millennia have treated these problems with rituals and spirituality (van Gennep, as cited in Turner, 1969). These treatments are, essentially, the basis of *Jungian analytical psychology*. The healer helps the client integrate their spiritual, ancient brain into conscious thought because it is wiser and less prone to loss of meaning. Guiding clients through the process of "individuation" as it is called, is a unique privilege (Jung, 1969). Through this process your two brains become one rather than just the conscious ego that you are aware of.

Individuation involves becoming self-aware, listening to whispered thoughts, dreams, and other unconscious messages, and allowing them to guide and transform you (Jung, 1968b). By becoming a more authentic version of yourself, you find meaning and allow the ancient brain to guide you and give your life a deeper purpose that your modern brain may not provide (Jung, 1968b). Transformation is what eventually happens, because your perspective is what needs to change. Usually, it is nothing dramatic: just a shift in perspective and a flood of images and emotions as the change takes hold (Kross et al., 2014). The smallest of changes can make a big difference to a person's attitude, career, and especially relationships. A person who is living an inner-guided life is not walking alone anymore, and so they are filled with purpose, imagination, and heart-mind balance (Jung, 1968b).

When a client seeks help, I find that the initial dreams and imaginings they report almost always point toward the problem itself: addiction, bad karma, loss of meaning, poor relationships, boiling anger and more. With their consent, I will deliberately invite a response from the client's inner beloved in order to help us both see the problem together. The inner beloved speaks in the language of metaphor, so any dreams, fantasies, strange ideas, or stories tell the tale of their woes in symbolic form (Jung, 1968c; Hollis, 2009).

Dreams and imaginings usually point to the problem symbolically. Some people who try to do individuation by themselves get stuck in half-measures while trying to integrate their ancient brain with their modern ego.

The fact is, no one is ever finished with *shadow integration,* and even the most enlightened people make mistakes. Most modern problems are associated with a lack of a proper relationship to the inner self (Hollis, 2009). Since there is no cultural training in this area, most people have no idea that the inner beloved even exists, much less that they should have a relationship with it.

Without an inner relationship, people tend to bypass everything related to the ancient brain: emotions, spirituality, wisdom, family connections, *inner narrative,* intimacy, boundaries. Such people are prone to *somatic* symptoms that mirror their lack of connection: migraines, fatigue, muscle tension, anxiety (van der Kolk, 2014). The lack of inner connection causes loneliness and isolation or feelings of disconnection even when there are other people around. Having a relationship with the inner self means you are never alone. Without an inner guide to talk to, all people have is their own conscious ego, and so they overthink things, which results in paralyzing doubt and poor decision-making (Brown & Ryan, 2003).

Inner guidance is fundamentally a personal spiritual experience, which Jung (1932) called an inner, experiential attitude, where you worship your inner relationship, but not as a religion. People who have a poor inner relationship will compulsively seek external possessions (money, status, etc.) that often lead to a shallow, unsatisfying life. These "things" cannot compensate for the lack of meaning in people's lives, however, and so when they reach the goal, they often feel empty and disillusioned, because they did not satisfy their deeper spiritual hunger (Jung, 1932). Outer achievement can seem as empty as the void of interstellar space because these things have little significance to the soul (Wilber, 2000).

People lacking an inner narrative or relationship to their inner self often have an ego that is out of alignment with their unconscious mind. This can lead to emotional distress, difficulty setting boundaries, and various psychological struggles. The goal is not simply to strengthen and re-align the ego, but to cultivate a disciplined conscious self that harmonizes with the deeper inner self (Hollis, 2009; Jung, 1968c; Siegel, 2012).

The most accurate perspective acknowledges the brain as one integrated, adaptive system that interacts with the body's nervous system (Damasio, 2018). This book is focused on the unification of our ancient limbic brain, with all its creative symbols, with our more modern cerebral cortex, with all its logic. Unifying those two is the process of being guided from within.

If being guided from within worked for your ancestors without any modern technology, it can work for you too. With all the noise from social media, however, it takes more effort to quiet the mind and focus the spirit. Everyone has an ancient, inner beloved, and a modern, egoic brain. Every individual problem has a unique solution that can involve dialogue between your modern ego and the various parts of your inner beloved.

What Is Our Inner Beloved?

Imagine a time over 150,000 years ago, deep in Africa, when a woman lived whom scientists now call "Mitochondrial Eve." She was not the only woman alive, but she was the one who passed down her mitochondrial DNA, in an unbroken lineage, to every human living today (Cann, Stoneking, & Wilson, 1987). Her legacy is profound, not just in our genes, but in the very architecture of our minds.

At that time, the human brain had already evolved complex structures over millions of years. Popular psychology often describes this layered architecture as the "triune brain," which divides the brain into the ancient reptilian brain, the limbic system, and the neocortex. The ancient brain is responsible for our survival functions, like heartbeat, breathing, and the fight-or-flight response. It is wrapped by the limbic and related systems, which support emotions, memories, and relationships. The neocortex is the modern brain that governs higher thinking functions associated with thought, language, and abstract reasoning, marking the dawn of culture and civilization (MacLean, 1990). Though simplified, this model serves well as a metaphor for understanding our layered psyche. Modern neuroscience shows that our mental functions are integrated into a single conscious awareness, but the brain is made up of at least three different parts.

These various parts of the human brain are integrated via a filter that Tor Norretranders (1991) calls the "user illusion." Our conscious self makes sense of the world through this filter, which integrates and simplifies the vast and complex subconscious processing happening beneath our awareness. Experiencing this illusion provides us with a manageable, though incomplete, representation of reality. Through the user illusion, much of what shapes our experience is hidden, including the messages from deep within ourselves.

As time passed, the neocortex, especially the prefrontal cortex, began to evolve. This "modern" brain fell out of harmony with the older structures. The ancient, less conscious mind, what Jung (1969) termed the primordial mind, holds deep *archetypes,* such as the shadow, *anima/animus, Self,* and others. These archetypes manifest themselves as instinctive human behaviors. These universal patterns shape our dreams, myths, and fears that echo through every culture and era. Such patterns of thought are the psychic inheritance of countless generations of human beings, forged in the fires of survival and social living (MacLean, 1990; Cann, Stoneking, & Wilson, 1987).

As the influence of the modern brain grew, humans faced the challenge of integrating this rational mind with its instinctive, symbolic core. The old brain felt, sang, created, and imagined; the new brain thought and planned (Herculano-Houzel, 2017; Gunz, Neubauer, Maureille, & Hublin, 2018). Sometimes, these two brains clashed, giving rise to anxiety, obsession, and self-doubt. To bridge this gap, humans spontaneously invented rites and rituals that initiated children into adulthood and united logical reasoning with instinctive experience (Legare & Souza, 2020). Archaeological evidence for symbolic rituals begins from roughly 70,000 to 100,000 years ago.

Cultural practices, like dancing, singing, and spiritual ceremonies, united the logical mind with the instinctive brain, creating moments of shared meaning and transcendence. Adults in the community learned, with the help of the local shaman, to merge their hearts with their minds to form a kind of wisdom that modern life no longer seems to possess.

These rituals were more than tradition; they were what I call "technology for the soul," helping individuals and groups reconcile the burdens and gifts of their dual heritage from their two brains. These rites offered a way to honor the ancient archetypes while giving space for the new, logical self to emerge.

From Mitochondrial Eve onward, our brains have carried both the wisdom of the ages and the promise of the future. Her legacy is not only in our cells, but in the stories we tell, the symbols we dream, and the rituals we perform to help make sense of what it means to be human. We need to break out of the user illusion that hides these quiet messages and listen closely to the wiser parts of ourselves.

The *inner beloved* is the messenger from my inner self. My inner beloved came to me in a dream after I started writing this book and suggested that it should be a series of wise lessons. The exact definition of what the inner beloved is (soul, shadow, spirit, anima, animus, or archetype) is less important than the messages it delivers. How your inner beloved delivers the message to you depends on how it manages to get your attention. Staying self-aware so you can receive these messages is your first step towards authenticity. Making changes from the inside out, rather than from the outside in, is how real change happens. As I explain later, actual change is accomplished by being, not doing. Changes come from within and transform your entire being. The path you walk with your inner beloved is your own unique, lifelong journey through the spiral maze of your mind.

The Dangers of Perfectionism

Many clients are trying to become better, more perfect versions of themselves. I have noticed that young people, in particular, try to validate their self-worth by projecting a perfect *persona* onto the world in order to silence their inner critics. Young people are so beautiful, of course, but behind all that grooming and those carefully curated Instagram posts lies the uncomfortable truth: life is terribly imperfect and sometimes tragic.

Jung (1958) famously pointed out that perfection is always hopelessly incomplete and leads to a psychological dead end. The individual may strive for perfection, but will suffer for their intentions (Jung, 1968a). The pressure of perfectionism causes neurosis in the form of anxiety, depression, obsession, panic attacks, and so on (Frost & Marten, 1990; Hewitt & Flett, 1991; Woodman, 1982). It is simply not possible for human beings to achieve perfection in the physical world. Anyone who believes in perfection is in for a rude awakening when the imperfect universe crashes down upon them.

The relentless pursuit of flawlessness not only causes stress but also, paradoxically, low performance. Perfectionists typically have rigid standards, causing doubt and fear of failure, which actually hinder accomplishment (Park et al., 2020). Clients are then trapped in a cycle where their need for achievement drives procrastination, self-criticism, and burnout, which prevents achievement. The way forward is an acceptance of imperfection and a balanced pursuit of excellence rooted in self-compassion (Sirois & Giguère, 2023).

Life often seems to demand perfection. But we cannot accomplish the impossible; instead need to navigate these challenges like water that finds its way through a lonely canyon. We cannot stay forever young, beautiful, and strong. But we can grow beyond our limitations through personal transformation. This is why collective archetypes exist in the unconscious minds of all people: to help us transform and overcome obstacles when the rational ego sees no way forward. Instead of perfection, your inner beloved will help you find self-acceptance and transcendence.

Having said all this, allow me to admit candidly that not everything in this (or any) publication will work for you. Perfection is an illusion. A flawed or false statement, however, does not invalidate the whole thing. We are all imperfect and contradictory, usually without realizing it. I have friends with significant problems who have given me life-changing advice. I have found wonderful ideas embedded in terrible books riddled with dreadful writing and poor reasoning. I can appreciate and learn from a beautiful work of art made by someone I may not like or approve of. This is where the ego and its logic can overlook great ideas through a lack of openness and personal bias.

    Certain parts of this book will resonate with some readers and not with others. You will find your own path by gathering the wisdom that speaks to you and moves you forward to live a more beautiful, balanced life in harmony with your inner beloved.

    Namaste,

    Scott Smith
    May, 2025

References

Brown, K. W., & Ryan, R. M. (2003). The benefits of being present: Mindfulness and its role in psychological well-being. *Journal of Personality and Social Psychology*, 84(4), 822–848.

Cann, R. L., Stoneking, M., & Wilson, A. C. (1987). Mitochondrial DNA and human evolution. *Nature*, 325(6099), 31-36. https://doi.org/10.1038/325031a0

Casey, B. J., Jones, R. M., & Hare, T. A. (2008). The adolescent brain. *Annals of the New York Academy of Sciences*, 1124(1), 111-126.

Damasio, A. (2018). *The strange order of things: Life, feeling, and the making of cultures*. Pantheon Books.

Eliade, M. (1958). *Rites and symbols of initiation: The mysteries of birth and rebirth* (W. R. Trask, Trans.). Harper & Row.

Frost, R. O., & Marten, P. (1990). Perfectionism and evaluative threat. *Cognitive Therapy and Research*, 14(6), 559-572.

Gunz, P., Neubauer, S., Maureille, B., & Hublin, J. J. (2018). Brain development after birth differs between Neandertals and modern humans. *Current Biology*, 28(20), 3359-3365.e4. https://doi.org/10.1016/j.cub.2018.08.033

Herculano-Houzel, S. (2017). *The human advantage: A new understanding of how our brain became remarkable*. MIT Press.

Hewitt, P. L., & Flett, G. L. (1991). Perfectionism in the self and social contexts: Conceptualization, assessment, and association with psychopathology. *Journal of Personality and Social Psychology*, 60(3), 456-470.

Hollis, J. (2009). *Living the examined life: Wisdom for the second half of the journey*. New World Library.

Jung, C. G. (1932). *The Religious Function of the Psyche*. In *The Collected Works of C. G. Jung, Volume 11: Psychology and Religion: West and East.*

Jung, C. G. (1936, October 4). [Interview]. New York Times.

Jung, C. G. (1958). *Answer to Job* (R. F. C. Hull, Trans.). Princeton University Press. (Original work published 1952) (Collected Works, Vol. 11, 620).

Jung, C. G. (1968a). *Aion: Researches into the phenomenology of the Self* (R. F. C. Hull, Trans.). Princeton University Press. (Original work published 1951) (Collected Works, Vol. 9, Part 2, 123)

Jung, C. G. (1968b). *Conscious, unconscious, and individuation* (R. F. C. Hull, Trans.). In H. Read et al. (Eds.), The collected works of C.G. Jung (Vol. 9).

Jung, C. G. (1968c). *The structure and dynamics of the psyche* (Collected Works, Vol. 8). Princeton University Press.

Jung, C. G. (1969). *The archetypes and the collective unconscious* (R. F. C. Hull, Trans.). In H. Read, M. Fordham, & G. Adler (Eds.), The collected works of C. G. Jung: Vol. 9, Part 1 (pp. 3-41). Princeton University Press. (Original work published 1959).

Kross, E., et al. (2014). Perspective change and emotion regulation. NIH Public Access.

Legare, C. H., & Souza, A. L. (2020). Ingredients of 'rituals' and their cognitive underpinnings. *Philosophical Transactions of the Royal Society B: Biological Sciences*, 375(1805), Article 20190469. https://doi.org/10.1098/rstb.2019.0469

Moore, T. (1992). *Care of the soul: A guide for cultivating depth and sacredness in everyday life*. HarperPerennial.

MacLean, P. D. (1990). *The triune brain in evolution: Role in paleocerebral functions*. Plenum Press.

Norretranders, T. (1998). *The user illusion: Cutting consciousness down to size.* Viking.

Park, Y., Heo, C., Kim, J. S., Rice, K. G., & Kim, Y.-H. (2020). How does perfectionism affect academic achievement? Examining the mediating role of accurate self-assessment. *International Journal of Psychology*, 55(6), 936-940. https://doi.org/10.1002/ijop.12659

Price, J. L., & Friston, K. J. (2019). Cortico-limbic interactions mediate adaptive and maladaptive behaviors. *Biological Psychiatry*, 86(10), 730-731

Siegel, D. J. (2012). *The developing mind: How relationships and the brain interact to shape who we are* (2nd ed.). Guilford Press.

Singer, J. (1994). *Boundaries of the soul: The practice of Jung's psychology* (Rev. ed.). Anchor Books.

Sirois, F. M., & Giguère, B. (2023). The mediating role of self-compassion and repetitive negative thinking in the relationship between perfectionism and psychological distress. *Personality and Individual Differences*, 204, 112058. https://doi.org/10.1016/j.paid.2023.112058.

Stein, M. (1998). *Jung's map of the soul: An introduction*. Open Court.

Turner, V. (1969). *The ritual process: Structure and anti-structure*. Aldine Publishing.

van der Kolk, B. A. (2014). *The body keeps the score: Brain, mind, and body in the healing of trauma*. Viking.

van Gennep, A. (1960). *The rites of passage* (M. B. Vizedom & G. L. Caffee, Trans.). University of Chicago Press. (Original work published 1909)

Wilber, K. (2000). *A theory of everything: An integral vision for business, politics, science, and spirituality*. Shambhala.

Woodman, M. (1982). *Addiction to perfection: The still unravished bride*. Inner City Books.

1 Understanding Your Inner Beloved

> *"It is here, in the secret recesses of the heart, that the relationship with the Beloved takes place. He was always here, waiting to be born into consciousness. But we need to prepare ourself for this meeting, we need to align ourself to the inner vibrations of the Self."* – Llewellan Vaughan-Lee (1993)

The inner beloved always whispers to us quietly, in inner dialogues, in dreams, in imagination, in the rhythms of the body, in worship, in nature, in playfulness, and in art. There are two ways that we experience life: inner and outer. "Doing" things in the outer world means activities, like diet, exercise, relationships, business, etc. Outer life leads to dissatisfaction. Inner, soulful satisfaction arises from "being" through contemplation and by balancing heart and mind. This is what the Buddhists call the Middle Way, where nothing is extreme. The Buddhists remain centered between the polarities of politics, commerce, and relationships. They live their lives in conversation with their inner beloved, regardless of the form in which this presence comes to them. For one person, it may appear as a shadow; for another, as an artist. Your inner beloved is always with you, waiting to guide you (Jung, 1967; Vaughan-Lee, 1993).

Dreams lose their urgency when the inner beloved knows that you are not listening. You must gain the attention of this ethereal presence. Jung and others state that the unconscious has a divine nature, so offering a prayer is appropriate (Jung,

1968; Hillman, 2007). The inner beloved does not want to be worshipped, however, so the term *prayer** is not meant here in a religious way, but meant simply as a conversation or dialogue with yourself (Johnson, 1986). **Terms in italic are defined in the glossary.*

Saying a Prayer to Your Inner Self

I say a prayer to my inner beloved whenever I enter into a conversation with it. This is an inner conversation, a spiritual one, but not a religious one. The inner self is *numinous*, according to Jung, meaning divine, and prefers reverence from the ego, not unlike a student who is devoted to their teacher.
https://youtu.be/ujNrQfOVgyw

> *O heavenly Inner Self,*
> *Please receive my thanks for your guidance,*
> *Past, present, and future.*
> *Please accept my friendship with open arms.*
> *Please accept my apologies for my imperfections,*
> *That I may always seek balance and self-awareness*
> *In my body and my soul.*

The Parable of the Overflowing Cup

Here is a modern proverb that is told in various Buddhist and mindfulness traditions with the same core image: "What is inside the cup is what spills out when life bumps you."

The Master said:
"If you are to be my student, I must know what you are carrying."
The student replied, "Carrying? What do you mean, master?"
The Master explained: "In life you must always know what you are carrying. Here is my lesson:"
"Imagine you are walking through a crowded marketplace, carrying a cup filled to the brim. We are all carrying something. Suddenly, someone bumps into you, as often happens in busy places, and the contents of your cup spill onto your clothes, onto the ground, and even onto those around you. What was inside comes out, revealing what was hidden within your cup.
If your cup was filled with sweet nectar, those nearby might smile and appreciate its fragrance. But if it contained sour vinegar or something foul, people would recoil in disgust. And so I say to you that you must learn to carry in your cup the sweet nectar of life."

Life is much like that crowded marketplace. The bump, the unexpected jostle, represents life's inevitable challenges, frustrations, disappointments, or hardships. When life shakes us up, whatever we are carrying inside inevitably spills out. It is not the bump that defines us, but what is revealed when we are stressed. In other words, when life gets tough, the truth spills out.

So ask yourself this: What are you carrying in your cup? Is it bitterness or resentment that will sour everything it touches? Or is it gratitude, kindness, and love that will bring sweetness to those around you, even in difficult moments?

The moral is simple: Fill your cup wisely. Know what you are carrying. It is certain that life will bump into you, but when it does, let what comes out uplift and inspire, rather than harm or alienate. Carry gratefulness rather than resentment.

Carry love rather than hate. Carry self-awareness rather than pointless worry about the things you cannot control. What you carry within you should serve not just you, but everyone around you in life.

A Lesson: What Am I Carrying?

This is a self-guided exercise that helps people discover what they are carrying. https://youtu.be/ujNrQfOVgyw

1. Find a quiet, undisturbed place. Keep a journal in this place. Perhaps dim the lights, light a candle, burn incense, or do some ritual that marks your entry into sacred inner work.
2. Sit or lie comfortably. Close your eyes and let yourself relax. Perhaps refer to the *box breathing* techniques in Appendix A, and take slow, deep breaths. Focus on releasing tension with each exhale.
3. Imagine yourself in your favorite inner place. It is a place where you feel protected, safe, and peaceful. Perhaps it is a beautiful meadow surrounded by a forest. Or a moonlit night near the shoreline. Wherever it is, you feel at home and fully yourself there.
4. Notice the surrounding details. What do you see, hear, smell, or sense? Let this place become vivid and real around you.
5. Seek an audience with your inner beloved. Put it in your own inner words, but here's a simple example:

I seek an audience with my inner beloved. I want to know what I am carrying. When life bumps up against me, what do I spill on myself and others? What are my burdens? And what penalty do I pay for carrying them? What should I be carrying instead?

6. Do not rush. Wait in silence. Be receptive and open. There is no need for words or logical answers. What arises might simply be a thought, a symbol, a scene, a face, a figure, a

sensation, a texture, an object, or even a color or sound. Trust that whatever comes to you is meaningful and symbolic, even if it is strange or unclear at first. Remember that this is your unconscious inner beloved. Your inner beloved probably isn't used to having conversations with you. You may get an answer of total surprise, outrage, or anger. If you experience something negative, ask for a part of yourself that is in a better mood to answer your question. If the presence that answers you wants to take control, withdraw immediately and end the session.

7. Otherwise, stay present to receive the answer. You might ask for clarification. You might ask for a different way of knowing the answer. If you are confused, simply sit with the response and let it be with you for a while. Remember that this is about being, not doing. The unconscious mind operates more symbolically and takes time to comprehend.

8. Thank your inner beloved for any response. Express a willingness to continue this relationship forever.

9. Disengage and return to yourself. Say goodbye, offer gratitude, and imagine yourself returning to ordinary awareness. Notice your breath and body. Open your eyes. Perhaps make a record of what you experienced before you forget all the details as you would from a dream. Extinguish the candle or incense, or perform whatever symbolic act marks the end of your sacred inner work.

Remind yourself that life will bump into you, revealing what is inside. This practice helps you know what you carry and transforms it so that you can fill your cup with what uplifts and connects.

10. Reflect on what the answer symbolizes and how it relates to your life, moods, and the "cup" that you carry in the world. Remember that this is just a conversation. You can have as many conversations like this as you want. This is your own personal relationship with your inner beloved. What you say and do there is your business.

I have done this exercise with many clients and in many groups. What's interesting is that there are two different outcomes that cause personal transformation. Some people discover that they are carrying something harmful (often fear and resistance), and through the script, they often understand what they should hold instead (perhaps openness). Other people are dismayed to discover that there is almost nothing in their cup, and the advice I give them is to fill it with something.

We should live our lives with courage and conviction. As human beings, we will make mistakes, but we will also find our unique path as we move forward in our journey through life. No matter what your cup held before, it needs to be filled with something that can withstand the insults and misfortunes of everyday life. Good things to consider holding in your cup are connections, relationships, forgiveness, service, authenticity, self-awareness.

One client who said his cup was empty was afraid to put anything into it. I gently suggested that, perhaps, he should simply fill his cup with the relationship he had with his inner beloved. As for what he should do "in the outside world," I suggested that it matters less so long as he is serving a sacred inner relationship.

The deeper meaning of your life is the inner work that you do. If all you do for the rest of your life is to commune with your inner beloved and find better ways of being authentic, that is a good way to journey on your inner path.

Getting Unstuck

"The psychological rule says that when an inner situation is not made conscious, it happens outside, as fate. That is to say, when the individual remains undivided and does not become conscious of his inner opposite, the world must perforce

act out the conflict and be torn into opposing halves." – C. G. Jung (1969)

What all humans carry in their unconscious cups is their *shadow*, the discarded ideas, habits, and lost thoughts that did not serve us well as we matured. The shadow is neither good nor bad, but simply unused. To become whole and unite with your inner beloved, Jung (1969) suggests that we integrate our shadow. Otherwise, these suppressed thoughts come back and make us suffer.

Some of the smartest, most knowledgeable people I know seldom make any progress integrating their *shadow*. They spend hours every week studying, writing, meditating, reading, and yet they are still that same traumatized little girl or boy who can barely handle the simplest tasks of everyday life.

Masters (2020) highlights that true spiritual growth requires confronting and integrating uncomfortable feelings rather than escaping them through false spirituality or practices that promise quick results without authentic emotions. False shadow integration, called *spiritual bypassing,* is where a person studies and works hard to become enlightened, but fails because of ego interference.

Laozi in the *Tao Te Ching* (1997) suggests that you must "be" rather than "do." Doing is forced action, whereas being harmonizes with life's flow without the ego's interference. Doing involves ego control that disrupts harmony and leads to exhaustion and failure. Simply being allows you to let your ideas flow freely, rather than to construct them rigidly. Doing is how the ego pretends to control physical reality, such as going on a diet or influencing a partner. Being is how the inner self gently orients your spirit, gradually shifting your desires and choices from the inside out through practices such as meditation, creativity, and yoga. Being is a partnership with your inner beloved. It is an inner dialogue and an eternal friendship. Being is a special awareness and a source of symbolic healing.

Your inner relationship has very little to do with books, or gurus, or techniques. Many of my clients read a dozen self-help books a month, but all those books do not seem to help. Clients tell me they practice meditation and breathing techniques, and yet they still have panic attacks and dark nights of the soul. This is often a sign that no progress is being made. *Integration* of the shadow involves depth and connectedness to self, not quantity of books read or number of hours spent in meditation.

Truthfully, once you understand how to connect with your inner beloved, 20-30 minutes is more than enough "inner work" for one day. Too much time spent in the presence of your inner beloved can be overwhelming and toxic, just like any addiction. When I am in the flow of writing this book, for instance, I have to take breaks and bring myself back into the real world. Otherwise, I risk getting lost in the wilderness of my unconscious mind. You can spend time there, but unconscious air is not the atmosphere that your ego naturally breathes.

Being in a relationship with your inner beloved means living from the depths of your imagination outwards rather than from the surface of your ego inwards. You must breathe deeply the waters of your unconscious self and live in a state of creative play, inspired by and devoted to your inner relationship. Rather than studying someone else's stories, live your own *inner mythology* as an authentic experience of your soul.

I only read one book every month or two, but I read them deeply. I rarely meditate, but when I'm stressed out, I use breathing exercises. I have not bothered to study ancient mythology in-depth, but instead have studied my own inner myth using personal dream logs, looking for patterns. I have deliberately avoided reading about other people's inner paths to enlightenment because I need to focus on my own way inward. So should you.

Making forward progress on yourself is not found in a study guide. You won't find inner peace in someone else's methods, not even this one. You need to find and befriend your own inner beloved to become a better friend to yourself. This is not a goal to achieve; this is a way of being with yourself. You will aspire to be a better version of yourself every day for the rest of your life. And you will both succeed and fail simultaneously. There is no right way to do it: there is only your way.

My friend, Dana Scott, Licensed Master Social Worker (LMSW), shared with me that she rarely talks about spiritual bypassing with her clients because they are barely in touch with their own spirituality. Clients might, for example, bypass their anger about their difficult marriages by endlessly reading books on marital communication instead of having one honest, slightly uncomfortable conversation with their partners. Such a conversation will begin the healing process. However, reading all those books accomplishes nothing because the reader is rationalizing and basically ignoring their advice. Reading about healing doesn't heal you: healing is done by gently touching the trauma and feeling it. You must shed tears to overcome your fears.

You can live an authentic life and follow your own path, whatever that is. And when you're not living authentically, you end up lost, feeling anxious, depressed, or like you're moving through life on autopilot. What's tricky is that so many clients do not yet know what they want. And that's not a flaw. I think being lost is often the first signal that something inside you is asking to be found. Your important work begins with turning inward and building on the idea that your life is your own creation, not someone else's expectations of it. This gives you the permission and freedom to be your own authentic self. The things you create are a symbol of who you are becoming.

The idea is to "create yourself" in your everyday activities. Jung, in his "Two Essays on Analytical Psychology" (1966/1977), suggests that clients become their true selves by taking off all the social masks that block them from being who they truly are.

Many people are not even living for themselves. However, we must avoid seeking the *magical other* whom we project onto our intimate partner (Hollis, 1998). Rather than living another's life through expectations and obligations, we need to understand who we are living for, and meet our own expectations rather than someone else's. We need to start the process of living authentically for ourselves instead. Easier said than done!

A Lesson: Helping You Get Unstuck

Many people are stuck and don't realize it. They keep repeating the same patterns, making the same mistakes, and getting nowhere. One of my clients has been stuck for years. He said to me "No one can write a script for that." I said, "Challenge accepted!"

Let's try a gentle, imaginative process inspired by *Internal Family Systems (IFS) parts work,* to explore and move past how stuck you are, step-by-step. IFS parts dialogue is simply an imaginative inner conversation where you interact with inner figures, images, or situations that happen while you observe them in a wakeful state. https://youtu.be/Qg_btB--GiM

1. Relax and find your safe space. Sit or lie down.

Close your eyes or soften your gaze. Take some deep breaths, relax deeply for as long as it takes and imagine yourself in a place where you feel completely safe, calm, and at ease. This place can be real or imagined. It is a place that welcomes and supports you. You can go there anytime you need self-support.

2. Name and find the stuck part.

Bring your attention inward and gently sense if there is a part of you that is stuck right now. This might be a feeling, a sensation, a memory, or an image. You can give this part a name or symbol, even if it only feels like "the stuck part," a heavy weight, a fog, a person, or something else that is meaningful to you.

3. Choose your symbolic tool to get unstuck.

Imagine that you can open your shed and pick up a tool to help you move or break through your stuck situation. It might be a shovel, a hammer, a key, a fire, a light, or a symbol. Choose what feels right to you. Notice what tool calls to you and take hold of it in your mind's eye. Keep the unblocking tool with you in case you need it later.

4. Dialogue between your compassionate self and the stuck part.

Invite your compassionate inner self, that kind, curious and patient part, to talk with this stuck part. You might ask:

> *"What are you feeling right now?"*
> *"What are you trying to protect me from?"*
> *"How can I help you feel safe and at ease?"*

Listen with openness, allowing whatever the part needs to say. If there is something blocking you from this process, use the tool to undo the blockage.

5. Explore shifting roles together.

With your inner self, ask the stuck part if it might try doing something different. Perhaps it can relax its grip or allow something to change. You can imagine using the tool you chose to gently but firmly clear space or break the blockage.

6. Sit with the situation and reflect on the why.

As the dialogue closes, allow yourself to "sit" quietly with whatever came up for you. This is like deciphering the symbols of a dream. Be patient, even if it feels uncomfortable. See if you can sense why this part of you got stuck. Is it protecting fear, a past trauma, or a lost part of yourself? Accept what arises in you without judgment. Acceptance is the first step towards healing.

Remember that this process is about compassionate curiosity and gentle exploration. There is no rush or pressure, only your willingness to listen and engage creatively with your inner world.

References

Hillman, J. (2007). *Anima: An anatomy of a personified notion* (with excerpts from the writings of C. G. Jung and original drawings by Mary Vernon). Spring Publications, Inc.

Hollis, J. (1998). *The Eden Project: In search of the magical other*. Inner City Books.

Hollis, J. (2005). *What matters most: Living a more considered life*. Gotham Books.

Johnson, R. A. (1986). *Inner work: Using dreams and active imagination for personal growth*. Harper & Row.

Jung, C. G. (1966/1977). *Two essays on analytical psychology* (2nd ed., rev. and augmented; R. F. C. Hull, Trans.). In H. Read, M. Fordham, & G. Adler (Eds.), The collected works of C. G. Jung (Vol. 7). Princeton University Press.

Jung, C. G. (1967). *Symbols of transformation: An analysis of the prelude to a case of schizophrenia* (R. F. C. Hull, Trans.). Princeton University Press. (Original work published 1912) (Collected Works of C. G. Jung, Vol. 5).

Jung, C. G. (1968). *The archetypes and the collective unconscious* (R. F. C. Hull, Trans.). In H. Read, M. Fordham, & G. Adler (Eds.), The collected works of C. G. Jung: Vol. 9, Part 1 (pp. 3-41). Princeton University Press. (Original work published 1959).

Jung, C. G. (1969). *Aion: Researches into the phenomenology of the self* (R. F. C. Hull, Trans.; 2nd ed., Vol. 9, Part II). Princeton University Press. (Original work published 1951)

Kegan, R. (1982). *The evolving self: Problem and process in human development*. Harvard University Press.

Laozi. (1997). *Tao Te Ching* (S. Mitchell, Trans.). Harper Perennial. (Original work published ca. 6th century BCE).

Masters, R. A. (2010). *Spiritual bypassing: When spirituality disconnects us from what really matters*. North Atlantic Books.

Vaughan-Lee, L. (1993). *The bond with the Beloved: The mystical relationship of the lover and the Beloved*. Golden Sufi Center.

2 Making the Invitation

"Close your eyes. Fall in love. Stay there." – Rumi

The central idea behind making an invitation is that your inner beloved is always with you, present since before you were conscious of yourself (Vaughan-Lee, 1993). You, the reader, are the ego. But as discussed previously, ego is there to organize your thoughts. Its role is to focus, to frame experiences, to create persona, relationships, and order; these are things we continually strive to improve. The ego is important in Jungian psychology, but it is just the part of yourself that is self-aware. Below the surface there is much more of you that you are unaware of. You need to make friends with the rest of you (Johnson, 1986; Hollis, 1993).

One approach I use is to make an invitation to the *inner beloved**. You can achieve this in many ways, such as through imaginative inner dialogue, or by saying a non-religious *prayer* to your inner self before or between sleep cycles. You can invite your inner beloved to visit you in a dream, or in those quiet moments when your imagination opens invitingly, like a door (Johnson, 1986). **Terms in italics are defined in the glossary.*

A Lesson: Helping You to Relax

The first step to make an invitation is to begin with relaxation exercises. I learned to use relaxation techniques when I was a child because I had asthma, and conscious breathing exercises helped me relax and ease the stress on my lungs. (See Appendix A for other relaxation techniques.) Here is a little script I sometimes use to help myself and others become relaxed so they can start a conversation with their inner beloved.
https://youtu.be/iDqxKG3ECNU

1. Get comfortable, sitting with your feet flat on the floor or lying down, if you prefer.
2. Place one hand on your chest and the other on your belly to feel your breath.
3. Imagine a gentle, glowing square or cube in your mind's eye, perhaps just in front of your nose. This is the box breathing technique. Close your eyes. Each side of the box represents a phase of your breath.
4. As you breathe in and out, move across the top of the box in your mind's eye, with one side for inhale, the next for holding your breath, the third for exhale, and the last for holding again.

Each time you take a breath, count to four, then you hold it for a count of four and then release it slowly through your mouth for the count of four. Allow each part of your body to relax, from head to toe. First your head, then your shoulders, arms, midriff, groin, legs, and feet.

Once you have relaxed, you are ready for an inner conversation.

A Lesson: Making an Invitation to Your Inner Beloved

Here is an invitation I often use with groups and individuals, which frequently evokes a powerful response. https://youtu.be/iAB4zFpNBpY

1. Quiet yourself, slow your breathing, and relax.
2. Make an invitation like this:

Divine inner beloved, Thank you for your constant presence. Accept my heart as an offering, A vessel open to your wisdom. Forgive my shortcomings As I strive for harmony and self-knowledge, may my dreams be a mirror reflecting truths I may one day understand. Help me interpret their symbols, to unlock the secrets they hold. Let me awaken to clarity, inspired by your divine guidance.

3 Have a conversation with your inner beloved about a topic of importance.

4 When you feel ready, let your breath return to normal.

Sit quietly, noticing any sensations or feelings that arise. Thank your inner beloved for joining you and carry this sense of connection with you until your next conversation. This exercise not only calms and centers you but also creates a mindful, loving space that is helpful for beginning your journey of inviting and meeting your inner beloved.

A Lesson: Meeting Your Inner Beloved

NOTE: If you have a diagnosed mental illness, or if you are simply afraid to proceed, seek guidance or companionship with a trusted person before attempting this exercise. Once you feel safe, it is okay to proceed (Johnson, 1986).
https://youtu.be/pqqqmpPqbMk

1. After box breathing and making an invitation, close your eyes and allow yourself to become relaxed and open. Imagine yourself in a beautiful place. Perhaps you are in the mountains beneath a blue sky, or at night under a perfect moon and stars. Imagine water, caves, wells, darkness, or depths, because those are symbols of the unconscious.

2. Manifestations of your inner beloved may emerge from these unconscious sources. They may be an image, a person, a feeling, a symbol, or some felt presence. Whatever comes to you is what is needed at this moment; this is the nature of the relationship between the ego and unconscious mind. The setting is safe, and you are in a listening, receptive mode. Your ego steps aside, as it should in such moments, and is used only when needed for listening and learning.

A word of caution: If your inner beloved appears as someone important in your outer life, ask your inner beloved to change its appearance to avoid damaging the real relationship with this person.

3. This is a time of being, not doing. being by the water under the beautiful sky in your imagination, communing with your inner beloved. As you sit or lie calmly, observe your inner beloved emerging from your unconscious. Its features will be unique to you. You may see yours with open arms, perhaps with fantastic features. Or you may see nothing but feel a presence. Walk toward your inner beloved and greet them.

4. If your image is fiery or unsettling, try to accept it or ask it for a less upsetting appearance. For most, the inner beloved appears as a peaceful guide, symbol, or felt presence. For others, it may be an unhappy figure, repressed or ignored, carrying anger or distress. Your inner beloved sometimes symbolizes the problems you are facing.

5. This is your opportunity to meet and embrace your inner beloved. If you encounter something frightening, try smiling, dancing, or singing in welcome. Your inner beloved

may not have appeared to you in a conscious state since you were young. As adults, we often lose touch with this part of ourselves; as we reach our teens, it tends to recede into the unconscious, merely sending us dreams that are easily forgotten.

6. The inner beloved may carry the shadowy traumas of your life, what others have done to you, what you have done to yourself, and the wounds inflicted by life, and especially relationships. Still, you can be with your inner beloved, making an impression and extending an invitation: "I want to dance with you. I want to be with you. I want you to be my guide."

7. Persistence is key. Just as it took Joshua from the Old Testament a long time to bring down the walls of Jericho, it may take time for you to dismantle the fortress walls around your heart and soul. Unless you are experiencing psychological distress, there is no danger in continuing these gentle practices. Relax, be alone or with a trusted friend, and accept whatever comes, whether it is play or talk. Fear is not the right response; instead, offer a welcoming attitude and a symbolic gift. Remember that your inner beloved is a gift to your ego: a way to never be alone again. With your inner beloved, you will always have a friend and advisor.

There are many ways to interact with the inner beloved. Some artists dance, light candles, or play their favorite music. Others draw, sculpt, or engage in creative activities guided by the inner beloved. There are countless ways to enter into a guided conversation with this part of yourself. Appendix C mentions the many ways that you can interact with your unconscious mind.

Your Inner Beloved Is a Companion

Remember, your inner beloved is part of your unconscious mind: it is less rational, less organized, but wiser and more attuned to the long arc of your life's story. Sufi teachers, drawing on the mystical communion with the divine inner beloved, embrace the contradictions inherent in the unconscious. Sufis focus on direct experience of the divine, embracing the contradictions inherent in the unconscious mind (Vaughan-Lee, 1993). I have learned to trust the wisdom of my inner beloved, recognizing that true wisdom encompasses heart, soul, and logic.

Jungian psychology teaches that we live in two worlds: the inner world of the unconscious and the outer, physical world of the ego. Modern society often overemphasizes the ego, but we are meant to live in both realms. Individuation, the goal of Jungian work, is about restoring a balance between the two by being guided by your inner beloved. The ego is just the visible tip of the iceberg; the unconscious is the vast, unseen foundation (Jung, 1964).

Most of who and what you are is an ego extension of the inner beloved that was created during childhood to help you navigate logic and relationships. But the wisdom of how to live comes from the ancient inner self, which is often left behind in adolescence in our very distracting, hyper-technological age. Partnership with your inner beloved requires getting to know this hidden self. You lived there as a child as you played and imagined in the schoolyard, but now you are wide awake: that relationship has faded.

However, not everyone loses their connection to the inner self. Artists and creative individuals often remain in touch with their inner beloved for inspiration and expression. For many, reconnecting with the inner beloved means never being truly alone. Sometimes, this presence is fiery or disturbing at first, until you resolve things together. This relationship with your inner beloved can be transformative, creating a "third body" in relationships or within the family unconscious (Zweig & Wolf, 1999).

My inner beloved appeared to me as a child as an "imaginary friend." We would talk and play and create and destroy worlds in my imagination. These days I am more fully conscious. I need to stay self aware, in touch with my dreams, and listen closely for the voice that gently guides me through my life.

Your guide is there, waiting for you. Your ancient brain offers wisdom that your ego seldom provides. When you find yourself overwhelmed by life, remember that your ego was never meant to handle everything alone. The best way to navigate the complexities of modern life is with the support of your inner beloved. That is the journey we are undertaking together.

References

Hollis, J. (1993). *The middle passage: From misery to meaning in midlife.* Inner City Books.

Johnson, R. A. (1986). *Inner work: Using dreams and active imagination for personal growth.* Harper & Row.

Jung, C. G. (1964). *Man and his symbols.* Dell Publishing.

Vaughan-Lee, L. (1993). *The bond with the Beloved: The mystical relationship of the lover and the Beloved.* Golden Sufi Center.

Zweig, C., & Wolf, S. (1997). *Romancing the shadow: Illuminating the dark side of the soul.* Ballantine Books.

3 Dreaming a Conversation

"The dream is the small hidden door in the deepest and most intimate sanctum of the soul." – C. G. Jung (1969)

In the darkness, dreams come to us as images and voices in the night while we slumber. Though we don't always remember them upon awakening, our inner beloved sends dreams to us every night to be observed in the theater of our minds. Each night brings a different stage with different players. We see friends and strangers, water and monsters, houses with doors everywhere with choices to be made on our path forward. The houses we dream of often symbolize our body and our inner life.

But many people claim they cannot remember their dreams. If you have not been paying attention to your inner beloved, it may not have been paying attention to you either. But if you ask your inner beloved for dreams, they will come. If you ask your inner beloved to help you remember your dreams, you will remember them. And if you ask for help interpreting them, you will find ways to remember and understand them.

Understanding your dreams can seem difficult until you realize that you can never understand dreams perfectly. The ancient brain is less logical and more intuitive and symbolic, so you need to interpret your dreams in terms of metaphor and symbol. And "figuring out your dreams" is not really the right approach. Dreams are from the irrational, unconscious mind.

Your dreams are not meant to be dissected for meaning. Analyzing a dream is like deconstructing poetry: a dreadful exercise that drains the magic and meaning from the words.

Dreams are best felt viscerally, like a story told to you when you were a child, in a suggestive state of mind, with emotion and vivid imagery. Your dreams are trying to send you a message. If you cannot quite understand your dreams, that is normal. There are resources that can help with the meaning of basic symbols, but they may send you in the wrong direction. It is usually better to "sit" with your dreams for a while, in contemplation, and see what ideas come to you (Johnson, 1986).

Intuitive types and depth psychologists are often talented at dream interpretation. Online resources can also help untangle dream symbolism and help guide you, just like your inner beloved guides you, to understand your dreams. You will be the ultimate judge, however, on whether the interpretation feels right. If your interpretation teaches you nothing new, that usually means that more messages from your unconscious will be necessary before the lesson is complete.

The Dream of the Nun That Changed into an Elephant

Recently, I was granted permission to use this beautiful dream as a lesson on how to understand and interpret the meaning of a dream and its symbols.

In my dream, I am a nun, somehow, and I manage to escape from a place where a terrible dragon was hurting me and chasing me. After my escape, I find myself in a beautiful park with trees and a lakeshore, holding a baby's bottle of water. But, at some point, I realize that I have transformed into an elephant. Although I feel relieved that I won't be recognized in this form, I start worrying that a single bottle of water is just a sip for an elephant. It is not enough for me in my new form. I look at the lake next to me and, just before I wake up, I notice a bucket next to the water. I wonder if that water is safe to drink.

The dream contains a lot of common symbols and images that people encounter. It is important to write down the specific details, with no elaboration, and see what they mean. You can do the same with conscious inner dialogue.

The dreamer is in her early 30s and grew up with strict parents. Since adolescence, she has experienced depression and anxiety. She has self-treated with some fairly harmless drugs, to which she has a mild social and physical addiction.

When we talked about what the dream meant to her, personally, she said it was a "call to her soul." It was so important to her that she eventually got another tattoo on her left calf of an elephant in the woods near a lake. But how can the two of us understand this dream?

There is a five-step process that I like to use for interpreting dreams and imaginings. You start with a *dream wheel,* do a simple interpretation, elaborate the interpretation with more personal reflections, start an inner conversation, and do a meaningful ritual.

Step 1: Using a Dream Wheel

Johnson (1986) recommends drawing a "dream wheel" with a circle in the middle and spokes coming out with each direct association that you can make:

- Spoke 1: There is a dragon or old demon chasing me, looking for me. Maybe these are my parents' values, trying to catch me as the nun and making sure I stay like a little child

- Spoke 2: The nun is my old self
- Spoke 3: I am holding a baby's bottle of water
- Spoke 4: I realize that I am now elephant, which is my bigger, wilder, more powerful self
- Spoke 5: There are trees in the park
- Spoke 6: There is a lake in the park with an empty bucket nearby

At the center of the wheel is the client's ego and her inner beloved, who seem to hide from the dragon.

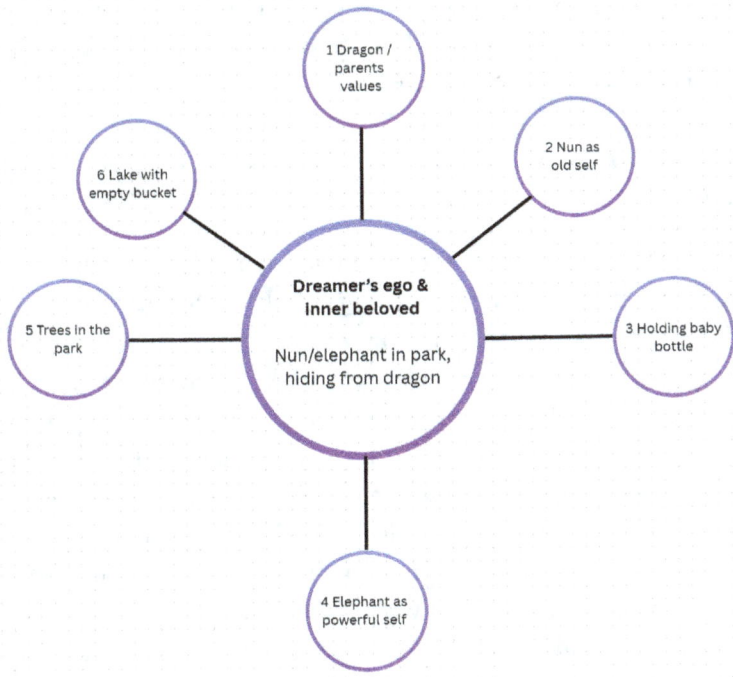

Image of Johnson-inspired dream wheel created using Canva

Step 2: Trying Simple Interpretation

To interpret any dream, you need to "sit with it" for a while and "be with the dream" to see how it feels. The primary rule with dream interpretation is that, until you learn something new that the ego doesn't already know, the dream has not been interpreted properly. For instance, when she entered the dream text into an AI dream interpreter, it returned this interpretation:

> *Your dream symbolizes a powerful transformation from vulnerability to strength and self-protection. Your concerns for sustenance and safety is your current situation. The safe park reflects emerging inner resilience and a cautious self-awareness of your growing needs.*

Unfortunately, she already knew all this. The reason she came to me was because she felt, strongly, that the dream held an important lesson for her to learn.

Step 3: Ornamenting Your Dream with Personal Reflections

After sitting with the dream and symbols for a while, however, we hit upon an interesting detail: When she was a child, there was an elephant at the zoo who had a baby elephant, but the mother wasn't producing any milk. So the zookeepers had to make a milk bottle and hand-suckle the baby elephant for a while. My client had always imagined that the bottle they used was a lot like the baby bottle in her dream. This reminded the client that, first: her mom and dad weren't very good parents and second: maybe she was a lot like that little baby elephant… still needing to be nurtured. This was a breakthrough insight that the dreamer was unaware of. The client is still a child and needs to be nurtured. Many young adults postpone traditional milestones, such as moving out, getting married, having children, or finding a career, so they can deal with them later, when they are ready, rather than rushing into things prematurely (Arnett, 2000).

It is tempting to conclude that this woman is trapped in a *puer aeternus* archetype. Developmental psychologists who study the maturation process of human beings emphasize that growing into an adult identity is gradual and can vary depending upon life conditions and opportunities for their *inner child* to mature (Sjöblom et al., 2018). People used to live fast and die young. Now we are living longer and growing up slower. It is not for us to say that the client just needs to grow up a little. Here, the client came in for treatment and her dream actually pointed to a child-like situation within her psyche.

When we discussed her association with the bottle and manually nursing the baby elephant, my client wondered if she was like that baby elephant in the zoo that she remembered from her childhood. She wondered if I was the zookeeper, and she was the baby elephant in her dream. She suggested that perhaps I was hand feeding her until she grew up. Naturally, I encouraged her to use her imagination to "drink from the bottle" of maturity and see what happens. Outcomes are often better when the client realizes the situation and helps themselves, with an imaginative ritual, to resolve the issue (Jung (1966/2014; Johnson, 1986).

At various points in the dream interpretation, both of us were using artificial intelligence (AI) to help us understand the various possible meanings of the symbols in her dream. But we both noticed that AI didn't provide any fresh, personal ideas about the dream itself. AI is a biased feedback loop that often tells you what you want to hear or what you already know. It is great with symbols, but artificial intelligence has never walked this earth, taken a breath, or had a soulful experience. AI is a digital creation that does not have to live with the consequences of its ideas or suggestions. Knowing what the symbols of your dream means is just rational spiritual bypassing because "knowing" is not a powerful inner experience.

Step 4: Starting a Conversation with Your Inner Beloved

At some point during a dream interpretation, I usually find it helpful to do an imaginative session or two . I like to relax, close my eyes, and have a gentle conversation with the images in my uninterpreted dream. With my client, we figured it out ourselves and then did some imaginative work later.

I guided her through a few imaginative sessions, where she "went for a walk in the park" of her dream. She had a discussion with her inner beloved about growing up and nurturing herself instead of being bottle fed. A few weeks later, she reported that she was experiencing less anxiety and depression. Then she told me about getting the tattoo, so we discussed the importance of the symbols she chose for the ink. When I gently asked her if she still felt the need for recreational drugs, she told me that only her new boyfriend still does that stuff. He's such a child, she said. As we laughed and talked, I quietly wondered if her dream had helped this young lady see herself as an adult now. The new relationship was a good sign, too. As I recall, she self-reported being alone before, because she didn't trust herself in a relationship.

Step 5: Doing a Meaningful Ritual

Rituals are simple, yet powerful, solitary acts that help you heal and integrate lessons from your inner beloved. Rituals are quiet, meaningful, prayerful acts that seal the integration of inner sacredness with outer experience. In the case study I presented earlier, I encouraged the client to simply "have a talk" with parts of herself in her dream. She was the one who came up with the ritual of getting a tattoo. Despite my own bias against getting inked, tattoos are an ancient way of marking the body when some significant event happens. My client used the tattoo to "make permanent" this important milestone in her life. The ink symbolized the moment she stopped needing to be taken care of like a child and stood on her own as a responsible adult. I'm probably over-simplifying the event, but that was my overall sense of what had happened in her mind.

    I had a powerful, transformative experience myself when my mother gave my father's class ring to me after he died. After I arrived home from Mendocino County, California, my inner beloved directed me to do a ritual with his class ring, which I kept in a little engraved stone box given to me by James T. Dove, founder of Prairie Heart Institute and past president of the American College of Cardiology (ACC).

Photograph taken by author, 2025.

    I got the ring out one day, said a prayer, put the ring on briefly, talked to my dad, and had an emotional breakthrough. The best rituals are very quiet, very personal, and highly symbolic. I felt profoundly healed. These days, my father and I have long talks in the sanctuary of my imagination. You should do rituals like that to heal yourself. Most people don't realize that they have the power to change themselves with imaginative rituals.

Being Persistent

The dream lesson earlier highlights that the secret to a really excellent interpretation is making it more personal until something new is revealed to you. This does not always happen, and that is why persistence is important. In the Old Testament story of Joshua, it says that the walls of Jericho did not fall in a day. But if you pace back and forth diligently along the walls of your psyche, staying committed and doing your best, the walls will eventually fall, and the inner meaning is uncovered, like a treasure (Johnson, 1986). No one expects perfection or major revelations every time. Sometimes, patience and persistence does not work, so you will need to try again with a different dream. There is a time for work and a time for rest. When the dream or waking fantasy calls to you, you must answer the call. The inner figures of your psyche want you to start a conversation. Say a prayer requesting guidance and allow yourself to be steered toward the answers that your soul needs. Remember, this is not a religious prayer, but a spiritual one that aims inward.

Doubting Messages About the Future

So what happens when you have a dream that predicts the future? The human mind loves to believe it can do all kinds of amazing things, but the mind is mostly good at telling itself stories.

There is nothing I can do to convince believers that they cannot predict the future. What I can do is point out some facts and encourage people to use their common sense. Hyman (1985) reports that some very respected and reliable researchers claim that certain individuals have an unexplained ability to know important things before they happen. Jung (1970) says that *premonitions* relate to human intuition, a basic ability that tends to "see around corners" and appears to defy the laws of cause and effect. However, most psychic phenomena are resistant to double-blind scientific verification (Hyman, 1985).

Science uses double-blind tests to expose bias and false claims. Everyone with a hint of intuition has sometimes felt like they could read the future. Human beings have been trusting their instincts for a very long time. Let your inner beloved guide you, but be cautious not to pretend that you can reliably know the future in detail.

I have received a few useful predictive messages from my inner beloved, and I have learned to act upon those only when they can do no serious harm. Usually, my self-awareness is rewarded. So, I advise that you act upon small, practical gut instincts. For example, if a dream warns you not to trust a new employer, you probably should not accept that job offer. Your unconscious mind probably picked up some warning signs that your ego missed. That is what intuition is for: to guide your daily life.

But if a dream urges you to invest all your assets in the latest money-making scheme, take a step back and consider the risks. Nietzsche (2002/1886) famously warned against trusting all of your thoughts, especially the grandiose ones. Messages from your inner beloved should be metaphors for your inner path, not financial advice for your pocketbook. People in this modern age of science are frequently too literal minded about symbolic messages from divine sources.

Just because quantum mechanics suggests that future particles can affect particles in the past doesn't mean your mind can do the same thing. Use your common sense to temper your so-called uncommon sense.

What If You Can't Remember Your Dreams?

It is common not to remember your dreams. The best advice for people who are frustrated because they cannot remember their dreams is simple: don't worry about it. The mere feeling and "sense of mission" that you get from a dream often gives people enough direction to proceed forward without the specific details. There are other methods that do not rely on remembering dreams to gain access to your inner beloved.

It is true, however, that recalling an entire dream and interpreting it can be quite healing for those who have the ability. If you want to remember your dreams, try simply saying a prayer to your inner beloved just before bedtime and ask to remember your dreams. Once your inner beloved realizes that you are paying attention, you will probably receive a powerful message.

You can also set a quiet alarm to wake yourself up early and see if you remember anything. Make a record of any details and try unraveling the symbols later. If you happen to awaken from a dream, don't get up immediately but instead lay there for a few minutes to recall it and then record the dream for future interpretation using the dream wheel technique.

References

Arnett, J. J. (2000). Emerging adulthood: A theory of development from the late teens through the twenties. *American Psychologist*, 55(5), 469-480. https://doi.org/10.1037/0003-066X.55.5.469

Hyman, R. (1985). The Ganzfeld Psi Experiment: A Critical Appraisal. *Journal of Parapsychology*, 49(1), 3-49.

Johnson, R. A. (1986). *Inner work: Using dreams and active imagination for personal growth*. Harper & Row.

Jung, C. G. (1959, October 22). *Face to Face* [Television interview]. BBC Television. Interviewed by John Freeman.

Jung, C. G. (1970). *The structure and dynamics of the psyche* (R. F. C. Hull, Trans.; 2nd ed., Vol. 8). Princeton University Press. (Original work published 1960)

Nietzsche, F. (2002). *Beyond good and evil* (M. Heidegger, Trans.; Original work published 1886). Harper Perennial Modern Classics.

Sjöblom, M., Öhrling, K., & Kostenius, C. (2018). Useful life lessons for health and well-being: Adults' reflections of childhood experiences illuminate the phenomenon of the inner child. *International Journal of Qualitative Studies on Health and Well-being*, 13(1), 1458235. https://doi.org/10.1080/17482631.2018.1458235

4 Being Guided by Your Imagination

"The first stage of active imagination is like dreaming with open eyes." – C. G. Jung (1960b)

Dreams are so difficult to remember that many depth therapists suggest more reliable, more conscious processes, such as *active imagination* (International Association for Analytical Psychology, 2024) and *Internal Family Systems (IFS) parts work* (Schwartz & Sweezy, 2020). These are imaginative inner dialogues where the client interacts with figures, images, or situations that happen while they observe them in a wakeful state.

Imaginative interaction with your inner "parts" is not daydreaming, which is passive; it is an active process that involves disciplined openness. It is not talking to yourself either, although that works too. There really is another within you, or several someones, listening and answering in their own way. The client lets unconscious material unfold on its own terms, but consciously enters into a relationship with it, asking questions, conversing, and interacting as an agent within the scene. It is not fantasy, although it might seem like it. The images that come to you are from your own unconscious (Jung, 1966/2014; D'Olimpio & Hughes, 2023; Raff, 2000).

Dialogue with your inner self is not exactly prayer, either, because it is not directed toward an external deity. Yet, like prayer, this imaginative inner dialogue involves reverence and respect for whatever form your inner beloved takes. It requires a creative openness where you surrender yourself to contemplation or mystical conversation. The focus in this process is on integration rather than worship: the client needs to recognize the message, accept it as symbolic advice, and incorporate it into their life meaningfully using creative rituals, behavior changes, daily practices, and ethical living (Johnson, 1986; Schwartz, 2021).

Hannah (1976) describes active imagination as a potentially transformative conversation between the ego and "autonomous unconscious figures" while the client holds dual awareness. These inner characters are parts of the psyche that behave almost as if they had a mind of their own. They are usually images of complexes or archetypes (such as the inner critic, wounded child, wise person, or shadow) that speak, act, and respond independently of your own conscious ideas.

The client and the inner beloved take part in and observe the unfolding symbolic material. This allows the unconscious material to manifest in the ego vividly and authentically. This dual awareness often provides crucial insight and healing that is *witnessed* and remembered. Hannah stresses the therapeutic value of this process. Active imagination fosters a dynamic relationship with the inner world and promotes integration through creative dialogue. This method of inner dialogue is an essential bridge in Jungian practices that deepens self-awareness and allows spiritual development.

Taking Cautions Before You Proceed

Doing active inner work dialogue is safe for most people with well-managed mental health, provided they feel grounded, and are capable of self-regulation. There are two situations where it becomes problematic. First, if the inner part wants to take control, and second, if you are not mentally/emotionally stable enough (Johnson, 1986).

You should not engage in imaginative inner dialogue if an inner part tries to "take control" or asks you to do things against your will. This is happening if you feel pushed, overwhelmed, or compelled to do something. The inner beloved should be in a more advisory role and allow the ego to interface with the outer world (Johnson, 1986).

The only other restriction on doing imaginative inner dialogue is that professional supervision is necessary for people who have severe, complex, or unstable psychiatric problems involving psychosis, suicide, or severe trauma (APA, 2015; Alloy, 2025).

Witnessing the messages sent by inner parts is important. You should not try to control your inner self any more than you should let it control you. The ego needs to be more like a reverent student: asking questions, staying focused, and learning at the feet of something far wiser and more ancient than itself.

It is also a bad idea to interact with inner images of real people that are well known in your real life. If you start treating the real person as if they were the inner image (or vice versa), this confuses the actual relationship by projecting your own shadow material onto them. It is simply better to ask for your inner beloved to change appearance (Johnson, 1986). Such suggestions are usually accepted..

Regarding IFS parts dialogue, Schwartz (2021) provides similar advice: stay safe and trust protective parts before accessing wounded parts. You should not put pressure on extreme protectors until you feel safe. Have respect for each part's role even if they are problematic. The active observer should gently encourage inner conversations with calmness, curiosity, and loving compassion.

This text uses a blend of IFS parts dialogue and active imagination, because I believe that active imagination lacks formal structure. Clients feel safer when there is a "script" and a goal as with IFS. But not every script goes according to plan, and not every script requires more than one part. It is necessary to stay flexible and ask for help from within or without as needed.

Talking to Your Inner Self

You need to allow your outside ego to be guided by your inner self because it is wiser. Otherwise, your life will be a surface-only ego existence dominated by "mere things." It is not that material things aren't important. But once you have established your own physical security, turning inward toward your soul is far more rewarding. There needs to be art in your life; otherwise, there will be no spark in it. Not professional art, but simply some kind of lived, creative expression that lets your soul speak, such as painting, writing, enjoying music, dancing, or any simple creative act that lets your inner life take visible form.

So many people walk the halls of conscious, everyday life, but they are dead inside, ignoring the imprisoned inner self. You need depth and meaning in your life that is not addicted to outer, superficial things. Worshiping the wrong things is what most people do: addictions to substances, ideas, behaviors, work. To interface with your unconscious in a waking state is a simple matter of closing your eyes and engaging with your inner self in a safe mental space. You can ask questions about a dream you had or some other burning question that your ego has that a generic interface cannot possibly answer. This process of seeking inner guidance is the beginning of your relationship with your inner beloved. Ego is an equal partner in this relationship. Although you are mostly seeking guidance, the entirety of your unconscious mind is unchanging and does not need any guidance itself. But the inner beloved, in whatever form or archetype, evolves as you do, through stages of enlightenment (Jung, 1959).

A Lesson: Having an Inner Conversation

In this lesson, I will use the "nun that turns into an elephant" dream from earlier. You should talk about your own issues, of course. https://youtu.be/JpFOiP48w-M

1. Lie down or sit back and relax. Concentrate on your breathing and relax completely. Refer to Appendix A for relaxation techniques.

2. Put your mind in the proper place. Here is an example I use frequently for clients:

Your eyes are closed and you are in a beautiful, safe place where you can be open and feel free. But instead of identifying as your conscious ego, you are a little more like an active observer. Your job here is to interact with your inner beloved as an observant student. You will not allow yourself to be controlled. You are here to accept what you learn here and integrate it into your conscious life sensibly. In your imaginary safe space, perhaps there are stars out, or the sky is bright and blue and the sun is shining. Maybe there is water or some other symbol of the unconscious nearby, such as a dark, secret place. There might be a forest nearby or something else that is full of mystery. The mystery is actually your unconscious mind. You are safe here, and this is where you can learn and grow, communing with your soul.

3. Open up your heart and your mind and make an invitation, something like this:

I call upon my inner beloved, that part of me that can answer the questions I have. Reveal yourself and come to me as my inner friend whom I can confide in and trust. We can sit together in this beautiful place and talk about the matters of my soul. Together, we can make our life a more beautiful thing.

4. The conversation begins. In this example, we are asking about the nun dream mentioned earlier. You should

replace this with your own questions using a similar tone. Just submit one question at a time, though. And take your time. There is no need to rush.

You sent me the dream where I was a nun, and I was escaping from danger. I want to understand why I turned into an elephant. Who was trying to hurt me? Where is this place, this park? Now that I am like an elephant, how can that bottle be enough for me? Have I become too big for my old, conservative life?

5. After your conversation, bring yourself gently out of your sitting or lying position and open your eyes. Take some time to make notes after the conversation. If something makes no sense, you can jot down further questions that you need answered to clarify your understanding. Try to avoid the temptation to do several sessions in a day. One or two is enough. Later on, you can have another conversation. When this topic of conversation becomes stale, just move on to the next big questions you have. There will always be further inquiries. There will seldom be perfectly answered questions. Not everything will be clear or cogent when dealing with unconscious parts of yourself.

Using Powerful Emotions to Heal You

Characters in our favorite stories often have emotional breakthroughs that cause a fundamental change in them as the story's journey proceeds. Strong emotional reactions are a sign that you are touching something important that can transform your perspective (Jungian Center for the Spiritual Sciences, n.d.; Chodorow, 1997; Cwik, 2011). Change is the goal of therapy, so having a breakthrough is what you want.

Earlier, I mentioned the importance of being an objective participant in inner dialogues. Yet allowing yourself to have a powerful emotional response seems to contradict the fact that you should remain objective in those conversations. This is a subtle but important contradiction that needs to be explained further.

On the one hand, you are in communion with your inner beloved. Being an *objective observer* is simply the ego withdrawing into an observing stance. This creates a safe, spacious setting where the unconscious material can emerge without being overwhelmed by your overreacting ego. This also protects your fragile ego from getting caught in unconscious complexes that can overwhelm it.

On the other hand, a strong emotional reaction during healing sessions is a signal that this topic of inner conversation is genuinely meaningful. If the conversation you have triggers a strong emotional reaction, you have touched upon something that is potentially transformative. You want that. The observer role is not a rigid detachment or numbness. Instead, it is a receptive, mindful awareness that allows emotions to be felt fully while maintaining a degree of objective clarity. You can feel something strongly and let it wash over you without getting swept away in the storm (Jung, 1968c).

Transformational change happens this way: you notice and accept the healing emotions that transform a negative complex into an integrated part of yourself. You are called upon to witness your own emotional responses with self-awareness, curiosity, and respect, without losing your sense of self. This is what therapists call "holding the tension of opposites." Anyone can allow themselves to feel something deeply. You become healed by also reflecting upon those feelings, asking questions, and trying to understand the lesson that your inner beloved is teaching you. That means being a witness to your own healing and continuing to ask meaningful questions even as the process is happening to you. This ensures a full integration of the shadow complex into your life (Chodorow, 1997; Krüger, 2025; Tozzi, 2023).

A *shadow complex* is simply a cluster of your disowned traits, memories, and emotions, that has taken on a kind of inner "life" of its own that reacts when triggered. A complex is part of your unconscious personal shadow that you reject as "not me," so it gets pushed into your unconscious and then projected onto things that resemble it. People who are triggered by controversial public figures find their emotions out of control. That is how people are "owned" by their projections. Once you accept and take back ownership of this part of your shadow, the complex no longer has a grip on you. This is called integrating your shadow projection.

If you need to withdraw because the experience is becoming too intense, or there is a risk of becoming re-traumatized, stop and come back to it later with a fresh perspective. When an inner conversation becomes too intense, some people try *journaling* or *self-talk* instead. There is a complete list of suggestions in the appendices.

Performing a Healing Ritual

A small, meaningful, and personal ritual completes the process of integrating the unconscious idea and healing via the dialogue. Rituals complete a session of shadow integration. Some of the simplest, most effective rituals involve burying what has died, lighting a candle, saying a prayer, making a toast, visiting or decorating a sacred place, breaking or repairing something, or blessing an important symbol (Johnson, 1986; Jung, 1964).

A good ritual involves small but powerful inner symbols. A bad ritual disrupts your life, such as letting go of your job or your major relationship. Helpful rituals heal and integrate your darker negative parts so you can move forward. Unhelpful rituals re-traumatize you so that you end up, months or years later, right back where you started (Johnson, 1986; Hollis, 1998).

It is the quiet, meaningful rituals that seem to have the most powerful effect on your soul. My mother gave me my father's class ring after his funeral. A few weeks after I got home, I felt a strong need to talk to him, but his outer voice was forever silenced. This hurt a lot, so I did a quiet ceremony with his ring to invite my father into my soul so that I could talk to him. We talk often, and this is a good thing for me.

In archetypal terms, the soul prefers to tread a spiral path rather than a circular one. The circle leads you always back to where you started with no progress or lessons learned. The spiral path leads your soul toward fresh places you have never been before. If you find yourself stuck in a painful pattern, you are traveling in a circle where no actual healing has taken place. If you have been trying hard to heal but find yourself stuck in a circular pattern, you are probably spiritually bypassing (Jung, 1964; Hollis, 1998; von Franz, 1996).

Rituals are best when private, personal, and symbolic. There are situations, though, where a strong external ritual can help disrupt a terrible life that needs to change immediately. I know friends and clients who were in dangerous situations who "blew up" their life and came through the fire brilliantly. This usually works better with younger clients who have the time and energy to start all over again, such as a second marriage or a new career. The problem is that you cannot run away from yourself. If the root of the problem, the inner problem itself, remains unresolved, the same old pattern will reappear, and you will have to try again. Recurring problems are the endless circle we walk. The people and places will have changed, but your inner situation is still the same as before.

It is better to seek a spiral path, because a spiral never crosses itself. Many people fail more than once before finally achieving progress. Interestingly, it is not the smartest people who succeed quickly. People who are talented at integrating their shadows are good with their emotions and have excellent intuition. For the rest of us, it takes longer to break the circular pattern and walk our inner *labyrinth* as a spiral path.

The people who eventually succeed in a spiral of success that moves them forward stay quiet and learn with humble reverence toward their inner beloved. It is not usually through dramatic outer gestures, but through quiet inner conversations that people are truly healed.

In summary, the key ideas necessary to make a powerful symbolic ritual while conversing with your inner beloved are: make it highly symbolic, deeply personal, and entirely harmless to your outer life. If you find yourself moved by powerful emotion after a ritual, you have probably done it correctly. This process ensures that you stay safe as you transform your inner life with meaningful but modest rituals (Johnson, 1986; Hollis, 1998).

What If an Inner Image Is Negative?

"Everyone knows nowadays that people 'have complexes.' What is not so well known, though far more important theoretically, is that complexes can have us." C. G. Jung (1968c)

First contact with parts of the unconscious can take on a negative tone because they have been ignored and trapped inside your mind for a long time. Jung (1960a) says neglected unconscious shadow complexes present as autonomous, hostile images. Van der Kolk (2014) confirms that premature engagement risks being overwhelmed. IFS theory calls this the "exile burden" (Schwartz, 2021).

Unresolved trauma will come to you symbolized as fiery, cold, unhappy, or very upset. Engaging with an unhappy, negative inner part can re-traumatize you. When an unfriendly or negative inner part scares you, it is expressing the results of whatever trauma you are suffering from. These figures literally represent the symptoms of what is wrong. Engaging with an inner part is important, but not at the cost of taking a step backwards in your healing process.

When you make a list of the things you hate about yourself and others, it is usually focused on negative things. But, to be whole, you must focus on a self-awareness of both sides, the polarities, or opposites. It is important to own your *projections* instead of denying them. Being aware of your darkness allows you to recognize and take off the masks you hide behind so that you can own your imperfections. You want to disown your terrible qualities, of course, but instead you must own them: for they are yours. So are your virtues. They are all yours. This is who you are, both you and your inner beloved. Be in conversation with your inner self to find and accept your authentic self.

When Jung (1960a) says that we do not have complexes, but instead they have us, he means quite literally that people are often possessed with a traumatized driving force. Our past experiences often traumatize us, and we live with an upset inner self that needs to be healed. But why are so many people traumatized? What is the advantage of a traumatized soul?

Strangely, traumatized people often experience significant positive psychological changes, such as increased strength, motivation, and an appreciation for life. Trauma, therefore, drives persistence and achievement (Teceschi & Calhoun, 2004). Such posttraumatic growth, as it is called, is not caused by the trauma itself, but by the struggle to rebuild your life, beliefs, and relationships after the traumatic event. Being traumatized or broken is not enjoyable, and the downside of trauma is personal suffering and adverse behavior that affect physical health that can often shorten life expectancy (Felitti et al., 1998).

When your inner imaginative parts are negative, there are several recommended strategies: change the image by inviting a different part, engage with parts compassionately, use journaling or self-talk instead, cultivate a calm, centered self that can "hold space," and use mindfulness and body awareness (Schwartz, 2021).

Asking your inner beloved to please change the image is a simple and effective way to avoid high-voltage encounters with extremely negative inner parts. I have found that asking for a less unhappy image usually works. Some parts are more damaged than others, so it is sensible to deal with the ones that aren't upset. Over time, the more broken parts can be engaged when the time is right. You can simply ask if they are ready yet, and they will tell you.

Think of your soul as a damaged porcelain cup that has fallen onto the kitchen tile. Most people's souls are shattered or partially broken as the years move forward. But you can mend the broken pieces of your soul with the gold that your inner beloved weaves and spins for you. In Japanese culture, this is called Kintsugi (金継ぎ) meaning "golden joinery." Your patched-together soul can never be perfect, but it can be made whole again with the inner gold provided by your soul (Johnson, 1998).

Image of "Kintsugi soul cup" Photo by Matt Perkins on Unsplash

Engaging the imaginative parts with compassion is not something that everyone can do, but holding and listening and crying with broken pieces of yourself works well. Sometimes, however, the level of negativity is too difficult.

Journaling or engaging in self-talk with your inner beloved will often reduce the "scare" index and allow the negative parts to emerge in ways that do not cause further damage. You will probably discover that the traumatized part is depressed, anxious, or obsessive, just like you. So it is wise to limit the time spent with these negative forces each day. Eventually, damaged and traumatized pieces of yourself start "integrating" with the rest of you and gain a fresh perspective that begins the healing process. Your inner gold mends the damage with stories and images. Don't ask me why, but this is how the mind works. Remember that a picture really is worth a thousand words. That means you should eventually switch back to imaginative dialogue once the parts have calmed down.

Creating a calm, centered self that can hold space with traumatized parts is done using self-awareness, emotional regulation, and mindful presence. It is helpful to use meditation, journaling, breathing and grounding exercises, compassionate self-talk, and visualization (Schwartz, 2021). Appendix A mentions ways of creating an objective observer part that is calmer.

What If My Inner Beloved Is Silent or Unnoticed?

Most books that discuss individuation fail to address the elephant in the room: what if nothing happens? Most adults do not perceive messages from their inner beloved. Those messages are hard-wired to happen in early-to-mid childhood and then the valve (for most) shuts off. Of course, some people who are predisposed, sensitive, or traumatized keep the channel open and continue to send and receive messages from their inner psyche. But for most adults, that channel is often closed or forgotten in dreams. But is it, really? Or is the ego afraid to open and acknowledge that channel for fear of what will spill out? A lot of parents seem to discourage their children's creative inner self from expressing itself. How do we reactivate our stifled creativity and inner conversations? Most people live in instinctive fear of their creativity, but living in fear of the unknown is not really living at all. The inner beloved is their unconscious "unknown," and knowing it is the pathway to healing.

The following subsections give you some guidance on what to do if the inner beloved has yet to make an appearance in your attempts at conversation.

A Lesson: Dialoguing with the Resistance Itself

You can have an inner dialogue with the blockage itself. I've asked many clients to imagine the blockage and talk to it. Often, I have suggested that they ask to "speak to the manager," because the guards at the gates of your unconscious are hindering the healing process. Strangely, asking to speak to some other part of your inner self works quite well. You end up learning who or what is blocking you (often parental symbols). You need to think of the thoughts in your mind as flowing water. Water loves to flow naturally in the lowest places. If you let your thoughts flow down into your depths, they will find a better path toward your inner self, rather than getting fearfully trapped running in circles. I believe the alternative to the "hero's journey," with all its battles and conquests, is simply a quiet, soulful path towards wholeness. With self-awareness, you can watch this happen to yourself and participate in your reunion with your inner beloved.

    I encourage you to have an inner dialogue and ask to speak to the resistance or fear itself. A client of mine did this exercise and told symbols of her resistance that she didn't need their help anymore. "You are wrong. You will break," they replied. Inner threats are a legitimate concern, so we spent several months working through the need for protection. Finally, we came to an understanding that protection was necessary, but the client needed to know what she was being protected from. At that point, her inner guide walked past the guards in her imagination and had a conversation with my client. Reasons and assurances were given, and the guards were convinced to put down their axes and leave the field of battle. Her guide handed her the keys to the gates of her unconscious and showed her the fear that they had been protecting her from. It was a powerfully transformative, highly emotional experience. Unforgettable. Fear is usually at the heart of most resistance.

    This aligns with how Johnson (1986) describes the ethical realization step of active imagination. Within a few weeks, my client had had a series of transformative experiences and was well on her way to shadow integration. She is still protected, though. Your inner beloved is always with you, taking care of you as best it can.

Clients often report feeling profound inner change, as if their karma or inner self has shifted. Jung (1968b) describes how what seems to affect the outer world are just projections of their own transformation becoming conscious. People often sense so-called *psychic phenomena,* such as synchronicities, that feel magical. This occurs as they integrate symbolic unconscious material. The individuation process transforms how they engage the world through expanded awareness, not merely changes in their perception. They do not simply put on different tinted glasses to see the world differently: they are now different from deep within their souls.

Here is a script that I use with clients who are receiving images of resistance. https://youtu.be/rLzm0htze24

1. Close your eyes and take yourself to a beautiful place in your mind where you feel safe and accepted. There is a sense here that anything that happens will be healing and emotionally vivid. Stay self-aware and reverent. Do not let your inner self take over, but instead let it guide you, show you, and talk to you. Help it like a student aids a teacher, by being cooperative.

2. Say a brief prayer:

Divine presence, guiding light on my path, thank you for your constant presence. Accept my heart as an offering, a vessel open to your wisdom. Forgive my shortcomings, as I strive for harmony and self-knowledge. May my dreams be a mirror, reflecting truths I may not see. Help me interpret their symbols and unlock the secrets they hold. Let me return from this dialogue with clarity, inspired by your divine guidance.

3. You are in this beautiful place. You can see the sky and the water and the stars or the sun.

4. Breathe in and out slowly. With each breath in through your nose, hold it for four seconds, and then breathe out slowly, releasing any tension in your body.

5. When you are relaxed and ready, open the door. Perhaps there are hooded figures, or guards standing at the gate, or a presence that looms and intimidates you.

6. You need to ask some questions, because they are blocking and resisting you. Try some of these questions.

Are you willing to leave your posts and let me enter? Can you explain who or what you are trying to protect? Do you understand that I cannot heal if you stop me from talking to my inner beloved?

7. Wait and listen patiently for any thoughts, feelings, or images that come to you. If nothing happens, try some other questions:

What is in the way of me receiving your validation and guidance? Do I need to forgive myself or someone else in my life that has created these guards that block me? What would that look like?

8. Take your time with this. You may need to do this dialogue more than once. You may need to do some creative journaling of this experience and ask better questions that are appropriate for your situation. Then you can repeat this and see what happens.

9. Think about what it feels like to be truly seen and validated by your inner guide. What messages does your inner self want you to hear right now?

10. When you are done, slowly open your eyes and come back into your body. Be sure to thank your inner self.

Dialoguing with Your Fear

Most people are afraid of their inner self because having these conversations forces them to be vulnerable and admit to the truth and their past mistakes (Brown, 2012; Rogers, 1961). This is why many people "hit rock bottom" before they allow themselves to be healed (Miller, 1991). The problem with hitting the bottom is that not everyone survives the impact. Another good metaphor for an encounter with unconscious archetypes is that the voltage is too high (Edinger, 1972). Many people would rather self-harm than face their failures (Linehan, 1993). And yet, interestingly, no one except you really cares or even knows about your failures and fears (Neff, 2003).

    You can dialog with your fear just like you dialogue with your resistance. Jung (1968a) says that courage is required to confront and integrate the shadow as a pivotal act in the process of becoming an authentic person.

    I had a male client who had committed a crime of violence that led to a quick divorce. He fell into addiction, was arrested, and eventually sought treatment through his country's healthcare system. After he got sober, he came to me with a vivid dream of being trapped in an underground tunnel system and being held against his will by a "mother turtle." I worked with his dream imagery, encouraging him to cut himself free with weapons if necessary, and confront this feminine image. We never figured out what the turtle symbolized, but once he could break free and confront her, his fear dissipated. We also had some discussions about how no one really cared about his failures except himself. Once he distanced himself from his crimes and the failure of his marriage, he realized that even his inner beloved didn't really care. We are all imperfect. The justice system dealt with his public crimes. As for his fear of failure, his inner beloved forgave him and even offered to help him become a better person. Strangely, because he was a bit of a criminal, his shadow was his good side, so it was easy to allow himself to take ownership of his inner gold (Johnson, 1998).

    For people who are traumatized, clinicians sometimes administer the Rorschach test to assess markers. Van de Kolk (2014) describes how PTSD patients superimpose trauma onto inkblots. Clients with serious trauma will see visions of their traumatic experience or have a total perceptual shutdown. The Rorschach and other clinical tests can help reveal unresolved traumatic memories and difficulties that clients have in managing their emotional responses (van der Kolk & Ducey, 1989). Managing trauma is beyond the scope of this book.

Being Persistent

In the Parable of the Unjust Judge, the Gospel of Luke tells the story of a poor woman who kept petitioning an unjust judge for justice. At first, the judge refuses, but he eventually relents because she never gives up.

Being persistent is important to combat internal resistance. Keep monitoring your dreams, imaginings, and creative ideas. Write whatever you remember from your dreams. Then apply the wheel-and-spoke method of the Dream Wheel mentioned earlier (Johnson, 1986). Life is difficult, but giving up makes it harder, not easier. People who are flexible in their approach to problem solving are often richly rewarded.

Understanding Your Tendencies

Years ago, I took the *Myers-Briggs Personality Indicator (MBTI)* and used the results to compensate for my lopsided thinking habits. That experience tempted me, while writing this book, to include an entire chapter on how readers could "rebalance" themselves based on test scores. Gradually, however, I realized that this is not how effective therapy actually works. Most therapists today focus on the specific struggles, history, and goals of the person in front of them, not on trying to adjust their client based on a test profile.

Contemporary approaches emphasize getting to know your particular patterns, wounds, and strengths. Therapists then craft a treatment plan that fits you as an individual. Your story, symptoms, relationships, and values matter far more than any four-letter code or score that you received based on your mood the day that you took the test (Pittenger, 1993).

That said, it can still be useful to get an outside perspective on how you operate in the world. This is like objective feedback that you sometimes get from people who don't know you. If you pay close attention, you can learn something useful about yourself and make whatever changes that you think are beneficial.

If you take something like the *MBTI* or the Big Five style inventory more than once, under different circumstances, you can gain an understanding of your usual habits and preferences. You can learn how you tend to think, relate, and make decisions. Just keep in mind that these tools describe tendencies, not destiny. Test results cannot predict any specific behavior. These test results merely hint at your style, but they do not define your depth, your soul, or the larger journey of who you are becoming.

The sun gradually rises on self-awareness. As you become more willing and able to accept yourself, both the good and the bad, you will begin to blossom like a flower basking in the light of your inner beloved. Acceptance of your imperfections is like an elixir that provides resilience, inoculating you against unnecessary suffering.

Journaling and Self-Talk with Your Inner Beloved

When you write or talk to yourself, your inner self is always speaking, especially if you write without editing yourself. There is an old maxim that you should "think before you speak." But with self-talk, you want to do the opposite and speak before you think. This allows your inner self to come through. Just listen to whatever comes to your mind and don't worry about how sensible it is. This will be your unconscious mind talking to you in its own way (Pennebaker; Ward, 2024).

The inner tone may seem depressed, anxious, or inappropriate. Set aside a small portion of time each day and express whatever comes to your mind and then review it later. It will seem like someone else is talking. This is accurate: if you write without editing your thoughts, you can read what your inner beloved is saying to you. You can start posing questions, perhaps one per day, and writing freestyle to see the answer. This process does not, per se, involve dreams, imagination or art. And yet there, before you, are the words of your inner self, talking to you.

You want to get into an inner conversation and be guided. If you start asking for advice in your journal or self-conversations each day, ideas will come forth, perhaps as creative stories. Then you, as the arbiter, can decide what to accept and what to discard. Remember that the ancient brain thinks in symbols and analogies that are often outside the culture in which you live (Lakoff & Johnson, 1980). You may not understand all the metaphors and symbols you receive in a message or dream. Clarification may be necessary. You are the student, and it is the master. Your inner beloved is not a literal thing. *You* are a literal thing. You cannot be whole if you are guided only from the outside, where you already live. Between the two of you, there is a whole person, a better version of yourself, waiting to be born.

So many clients think that when they finally integrate their shadow, they will become a very different person. This is not accurate. First, shadow integration is never complete. Second, the modern ego is too literal-minded, identifying with rationality while repressing the unconscious. Instead of changing completely, you become a more authentic being as the ego engages and unites these opposites through conscious dialogue. This synthesis, which Jung (1960c) called the *transcendent function,* causes individuation, which is the lifetime process of being guided from within towards wholeness.

Shadow integration transforms your relationship to yourself and the world, fostering greater authenticity and flexibility rather than a mere change in perception. Clients often describe this as "changing my karma," "becoming more open," or simply "being more self-aware." Jung (1969) explained that the Tao simply wants you to "become." What you become, once you have joined forces with your inner beloved, is a matter of the choices you make.

Using Embodied or Somatic Practices

The body is an instrument to do good works on behalf of your inner beloved. When you honor your body, your soul is honored as well. For many, however, the body is ignored and treated unconsciously. Highly rational or intuitive people, for instance, often couldn't care less about their body other than as an inconvenient thing that needs food and sleep and pleasure. There is a good reason for women to view their bodies as a monthly nuisance that is better ignored and denied. There is also a lot of unconscious cultural shame conditioning that makes women and men think poorly of their imperfect bodies (Brown, 2012).

Bringing your body into conscious awareness is an act of soulful devotion to your inner beloved (Woodman, 1982). Practices that help you notice physical sensations and movements, including symptoms, can help you discover what your body is trying to tell you (Stromsted & Levine, 2016). Your breathing, stretching, and the way you move are messages. Dancing, yoga, breathing slowly, and putting your hand on your heart help you express your body freely without worrying about how it looks or functions. Walking in nature stirs quiet reflection and interior response. These physical acts bring to mind emotions and memories that contain messages. Learning to listen to your body can even save you a trip to the doctor's office because you understand when it is trying to tell you something (Dunlea, 2019).

Seeking Professional Support

Obviously, some people will need more help. A therapy book is just a set of suggestions, and there is no direct penalty for not taking advice. There are paid professionals around the world who can guide you through these ideas in a different context. Some people need to seek a licensed therapist in order to give themselves permission to get better (Prochaska, Norcross, & DiClemente, 1994).

For clients who cannot or will not connect with the inner beloved, I sometimes recommend *Cognitive-Behavioral Therapy (CBT)*, because it is rational and based on evidence rather than inner metaphor. CBT cannot address the inner self, but it can help to improve your thinking habits. Using CBT will retrain your conscious self to avoid irrational worries, and that's a good start. Such behavioristic methods are appropriate for clients who are unable or unwilling to engage with inner guidance.

Consult with a licenced health professional if you are experiencing persistent depression, anxiety or other problems (for over two weeks) that interfere with work or relationships such as trauma flashbacks, or suicidal thoughts. This book complements, not replaces, professional diagnosis and treatment. Certified therapies or prescribed medication may be indicated. Your safety comes first (APA, 2023).

Working in Groups

Reading in a group and analyzing books written by experts can take the place of more expensive personal therapy.

Group work allows members to learn from others, share interpretations of the text, and support each other in the healing process (Johnson, 1993). The secret to success in groups is to have a good leader who keeps the discussion on track, ensures diverse views, and chooses books wisely so that each selection provides a balance of different perspectives.

Shadow Integration

Various Jungian texts describe techniques related to individuation or shadow integration. These books provide a specific perspective that can really help group members find the right way to approach and heal themselves. Some shadow integration writers have an amazing capacity to provide a perspective that avoids or encompasses both the masculine and the feminine perspective. This book approaches individuation as an inner conversation, where the readers do their own shadow integration in a conversation with their inner beloved.

Storytelling Therapy

Storytelling therapy is one of the most ancient types of therapy. *Narrative therapy* started around ancient campfires, with people telling stories and relating collective human experiences. Telling stories can be powerful if the narrative is compelling, and the examples are evocative (White & Epston, 1990). In fairness, however, vivid stories can also cause trauma victims to temporarily reexperience distress that could potentially retraumatize them. That is why trauma narratives need to be paced gently and held in a safe, supportive context (Schauer, et al., 1990). In the past, for example, I had bad dreams every time I watched a really great horror movie. The dreams stopped once I stopped watching scary films.

Symbol Interpretation

Participating in a group for dream or creative work can educate members about techniques and common symbols that arise during their slumbers. Artificial intelligence (AI) can help enhance the generic understanding of these symbols. Temple (2025) cautions users that AI provides general meaning but does not capture the personal significance of dreams. AI also often tells people what they want to hear, and it inherently lacks genuine human empathy.

Academic or Rational

Rational people prefer purely academic approaches that describe and define the concepts of analytical psychology itself. With a few exceptions, Jung's writings are highly academic because the intended audience was fellow psychotherapists that practiced during his lifetime (Stein, 1988). Highly rational approaches inherently bypass spirituality. Von Franz (1983/1990) voiced frequent criticism for the "men's club" of extremely rationalistic schools of psychotherapy that developed back in the early 1900s. This contrasted with Jung's more symbolic, soul-oriented approach, which was still one-sided in her opinion, but closer to a balanced, holistic approach.

Trauma-Based

Trauma-based approaches are quite helpful for the wounded client, who is interested in healing symbolically. Each book focuses on a particular trauma, such as victims of abuse, addiction, narcissism, PTSD, and so on (Tuley & White, 2023).

Creativity

There are creative therapeutic approaches that focus on art and intuitive expression, such as sand play, drawing, and ceramics. Symbol amplification is used to reveal the meaning of a person's inner myth. Some mythic books focus on the *mandala* symbols as a way of interacting with the Self (Ulanov, 1996).

Psychodrama

There are psychodrama techniques that reenact internal conflicts. Dramatic action, such as role-playing, is used to help participants externalize and act out emotional struggles rather than just talking them out (Gonçalves, Matos, & Santos, 2018).

Somatic Embodiment

There are somatic embodiment techniques that explore bodily sensations and movements to access and process internal psychological states. Since many clients are unconscious of their body, this approach emphasizes listening to the body's signals, such as tension, breath, posture, or movement, to receive the messages it is trying to send (Stromsted & Levine, 2016).

Summary

There are more self-help books out there to discuss than there are visible stars in the sky. Pick the ones that appeal to you and begin your own personal journey toward transcendence.

Appendix C lists common ways to receive messages from your unconscious mind.

References

Alloy, A. (2025, May 1). May 2025 *clinical supervision topic: Congruence, genuineness, and Internal Family Systems*. [Clinical supervision newsletter]. https://www.arianalloydlcsw.com/news/2025/5/1/may-2025-clinical-supervision-topic-congruence-genuineness-and-internal-family-systems

APA. (2015). Guidelines for clinical supervision in health service psychology. *American Psychologist, 70*(1), 35-41. https://doi.org/10.1037/a0037405

APA. (2023). *Clinical practice guideline for the treatment of depression across three age cohorts*. American Psychological Association.

Brown, B. (2012). *Daring greatly: How the courage to be vulnerable transforms the way we live, love, parent, and lead*. Avery.

Chodorow, J. (Ed.). (1997). *Jung on Active Imagination*. Princeton University Press.

Cwik, A. (2011). The Healing Power of Active Imagination on Posttraumatic Stress. *International Journal of Transpersonal Studies, 30*(1-2), 4-14.

D'Olimpio, L., & Hughes, M. (2023). Active imagination: A method of conscious dialogue with the unconscious. *Journal of Analytical Psychology, 68*(2), 189-210. https://doi.org/10.1111/1468-5922.12539

Dunlea, M. (2019). *BodyDreaming in the treatment of developmental trauma: An integrative approach for trauma therapists and clients*. Routledge.

Edinger, E. F. (1972). *Ego and Archetype: Individuation and the Religious Function of the Psyche*. Shambhala Publications.

Felitti, V. J., Anda, R. F., Nordenberg, D., Williamson, D. F., Spitz, A. M., Edwards, V., ... & Marks, J. S. (1998).

Relationship of childhood abuse and household dysfunction to many of the leading causes of death in adults: The Adverse Childhood Experiences (ACE) Study. *American Journal of Preventive Medicine*, 14(4), 245-258. https://doi.org/10.1016/S0749-3797(98)00017-8

Gonçalves, M., Matos, M., & Santos, A. (2018). The Core Techniques of Morenian Psychodrama: A Systematic Review. *International Journal of Environmental Research and Public Health*, 15(7), 1457. https://doi.org/10.3390/ijerph15071457

Hannah, B. (1976). *Encounters with the unconscious: The phenomenon of active imagination*. Princeton University Press.

Hollis, J. (1998). *The Eden Project: In search of the magical other*. Inner City Books.

International Association for Analytical Psychology. (2024). *Active imagination*. https://iaap.org/jung-analytical-psychology/short-articles-on-analytical-psychology/active-imagination-2/

Johnson, R. A. (1986). *Inner work: Using dreams and active imagination for personal growth*. Harper & Row.

Johnson, R. A. (1998). *Inner gold: Understanding psychological projection*. HarperOne.

Johnson, S., & Lee, M. (2018). Understanding self-harm behaviors. *Journal of Clinical Psychology*, 74(3), 345-356.

Jung, C. G. (1959). *Aion: Researches into the phenomenology of the self* (R.F.C. Hull, Trans.). In *The Collected Works of C. G. Jung* (Vol. 9, Part II, p. 70, para. 126). Princeton University Press. (Original work published 1951)

Jung, C. G. (1960a). Complexes (Vol. 8, para. 200). In H. Read, M. Fordham, G. Adler, & W. McGuire (Eds.), *The *collected works of C. G. Jung* (R. F. C. Hull, Trans.). Princeton University Press.

Jung, C. G. (1960b). *The Tavistock lectures* (R. F. C. Hull, Trans.). Routledge & Kegan Paul. (Original work published 1935)

Jung, C. G. (1960c). The transcendent function. In H. Read, M. Fordham, G. Adler, & W. McGuire (Eds.), *The structure and dynamics of the psyche* (R. F. C. Hull, Trans., pp. 273–300, paras. 131–193). Princeton University Press. (Original work published 1916)

Jung, C. G. (1964). *Man and his symbols* (R. F. C. Hull, Trans.). Doubleday.

Jung, C. G. (1966). *Collected Works of C.G. Jung* (R. F. C. Hull, Trans.; Vol. 12). Princeton University Press. (Original work published 1954)

Jung, C. G. (1966). *The practice of psychotherapy* (J. Hull, Trans.). In H. Read et al. (Eds.), *The collected works of C. G. Jung: Vol. 16*. Princeton University Press. (Original work published 1946)

Jung, C. G. (1968a). *Psychological types* (R. F. C. Hull, Trans.). In H. Read, M. Fordham, & G. Adler (Eds.), *The collected works of C. G. Jung: Vol. 6* (pp. 3-294). Princeton University Press. (Original work published 1921)

Jung, C. G. (1968b). *The archetypes and the collective unconscious* (R. F. C. Hull, Trans.). In H. Read, M. Fordham, & G. Adler (Eds.), The collected works of C. G. Jung: Vol. 9, Part 1 (pp. 3-41). Princeton University Press. (Original work published 1959).

Jung, C. G. (1968c). *The structure and dynamics of the psyche* (Collected Works, Vol. 8). Princeton University Press.

Jung, C. G. (1969). *Commentary on The Secret of the Golden Flower: A Chinese book of life* (R. F. C. Hull, Trans.).

Princeton University Press. (Original work published 1929)

Jungian Center for the Spiritual Science. *Jung on Active Imagination: Features, Methods and Warnings* (n.d.).

Krüger, R. (2025). *The definitive active imagination guide.* https://www.rafaelkruger.com/the-definitive-active-imagination-guide-by-carl-jung/

Lakoff, G., & Johnson, M. (1980). *Metaphors we live by.* University of Chicago Press.

Linehan, M. M. (1993). *Cognitive-behavioral treatment of borderline personality disorder.* Guilford.

Miller, W. R. (1991). *Motivational interviewing: Preparing people to change addictive behavior.* Guilford Press.

Mück, M., Mattes, A., Porth, E., & Stahl, J. (2023). Narcissism and the perception of failure –evidence from the error-related negativity and the error positivity. *Frontiers in Psychology*, 13, Article 1061547. https://doi.org/10.3389/fpsyg.2022.1061547

Neff, K. D. (2003). Self-compassion: An alternative conceptualization of a healthy attitude toward oneself. *Self and Identity*, 2(2), 85-101.

Perry, C. (2023). The Jungian shadow. *Society of Analytical Psychology.* https://www.thesap.org.uk/articles-on-jungian-psychology-2/about-analysis-and-therapy/the-shadow/

Pittenger, D. J. (1993). Measuring the MBTI...And coming up short. *Journal of Career Planning & Employment*, 54(1), 48-52.

Pennebaker, J. W. (1997). *Opening up: The healing power of expressing emotions* (2nd ed.). Guilford Press.

Prochaska, J. O., Norcross, J. C., & DiClemente, C. C. (1994). Changing for good: *The revolutionary program that explains the six stages of change and teaches you how to free yourself from bad habits*. William Morrow and Company.

Raff, J. (2000). *Jung and the alchemical imagination: Studies in the transformational imagination in alchemy and analytical psychology*. Brunner-Routledge.

Rogers, C. R. (1961). *On becoming a person: A therapist's view of psychotherapy*. Houghton Mifflin.

Schauer, M., Neuner, F., & Elbert, T. (2011). *Narrative exposure therapy: A short-term treatment for traumatic stress disorders* (2nd ed.). Hogrefe.

Schwartz, R. C. (1995). *Internal family systems therapy*. Guilford Press.

Schwartz, R. C. (2021). *No Bad Parts: Healing Trauma and Restoring Wholeness with the Internal Family Systems Model*. Sounds True.

Schwartz, R. C., & Sweezy, M. (2020). *Internal family systems therapy* (2nd ed.). Guilford Press.

Smith, J., & Doe, A. (2010). The impact of hitting rock bottom: Psychological risks and resilience. *American Journal of Psychiatry*, 167(6), 657-663.

Stone, H., & Stone, S. (1992). *Embracing our selves: The voice dialogue manual*. New World Library.

Stromsted, T. A., & Levine, P. A. (2016). *Authentic movement: Moving the body, moving the self, being moved: A collection of essays*. Jessica Kingsley Publishers.

Taylor, S. (2005). *The psychology of self-perception*. Oxford University Press.

Tedeschi, R. G., & Calhoun, L. G. (2004). Posttraumatic growth: Conceptual foundations and empirical evidence. *Psychological Inquiry*, 15(1), 1-18. https://doi.org/10.1207/s15327965pli1501_01

Temple, J. (2025, September 30). Does AI dream interpretation really work? *This Jungian Life*. https://thisjungianlife.com/ai-dream-interpretation/

Tozzi, C. (Ed.). (2023). *Active Imagination in Theory, Practice and Training: The Special Legacy of C.G. Jung* (Vol. 1). Routledge.

Tuley, L., & White, J. (Eds.). (2023). *Jungian analysis in a world on fire: At the nexus of individual and collective trauma.* Routledge.

Ulanov, A. B. (1996). The feminine spirit: *Dynamics of the feminine in mythology, religion, and therapy.* Routledge.

van der Kolk, B. A. (2014). *The body keeps the score: Brain, mind, and body in the healing of trauma.* Viking.

van der Kolk, B. A., & Ducey, C. P. (1989). The psychological processing of traumatic experience: Rorschach patterns in posttraumatic stress disorder. *Journal of Traumatic Stress,* 2(3), 259–274. https://doi.org/10.1002/jts.2490020305

von Franz, M.-L. (1983/1990). *C. G. Jung: His Myth in Our Time.* New York, NY: G. P. Putnam's Sons. (Original work published 1975).

von Franz, M.-L. (1996). *Shadow and evil in fairy tales* (R. L. Hall, Trans.). Shambhala.

Ward, R. T. (2024). *The potential of automatic writing as a tool for depth psychology.* [Doctoral dissertation, University of Depth Psychology]. ProQuest Dissertations Publishing.

White, M., & Epston, D. (1990). *Narrative means to therapeutic ends.* W. W. Norton & Company.

Woodman, M. (1982). *Addiction to perfection: The still unravished bride.* Inner City Books.

5 Finding Your Inner Path

Student: Last night I was up until 4 a.m. writing in a frenzy after I dreamed of my inner beloved. I wrote almost 100 pages!

Guru: That is wonderful!

Student: My friend is also a writer. But she complains that every time she sits down to write, nothing great happens.

Guru: This is because she seeks her words rather than letting them find her.

Student: What do you mean?

Guru: A wise person does not let their ego go in search of great things. Great things will find the wise person who stays open and self-aware.

Student: Oh, you mean that she is trying too hard to write something great?

Guru: Something great found you last night, and you wrote it down, didn't you?

Student: Yes! I was inspired.

Guru: Your inner beloved came to you and guided your hand to create something beautiful. Do not seek things. Let them find you.

The parable about how people "find" their inner voice is a great lesson. Seeking things involves your ego, which is prone to projection and error. The ego gets easily obsessed with something and starts seeing it everywhere, but it usually forces the issue and makes mistakes. Instead, if you wait quietly, using your observing self, your inner beloved will guide you to the things your soul needs to find. You cannot always get what you want, but if you are guided from within, you can find what you need. The great lesson here is: do not seek things, let them find you.

Not that you should sit passively, in the dark, waiting for things to come to you as if by magic. Instead, live your life and stay open and aware of your own thoughts. In this way, you can put yourself in situations where your inner beloved can show you the things it wants you to find. You are the eyes and ears that serve the purpose of your inner beloved. If you try to find something that is not within you, it will lack the spark of inspiration. This book was inside of me. My inner beloved came to me in a dream and asked me to write it as a series of lessons. He took my hand, showed me what he wanted, and I wrote it based on his guidance. That is how finding things from within is done.

Finding Creativity Versus Forcing It

"So the unwanting soul sees what is hidden, and the ever-wanting soul sees only what it wants." – Lao Tzu (1997)

People's egos frequently make a wreck of their outer lives by insisting on things being a certain way. One client insists on marrying the partner of their dreams. Another is determined to make a billion dollars before they are thirty. There is nothing inherently wrong with having lofty goals. More important than great aspirations is following their inner path, which is revealed to them. Goals without an inner source have no merit.

Some people will not listen to an elder statesman telling them what they can and cannot do. But a wise person can learn to sit quietly and listen closely, finding a path forward from their soul. If their inner beloved is not interested in making a billion dollars, it is unlikely to happen, and much suffering will teach them that lesson the hard way.

The path of water seeks the lowest points upon which to flow. Water does not flow upwards to high places. You find your inner path by turning your thoughts inward and walking in the low places where the soul loves to go. Stay low, where the soul resides, and walk with your inner beloved.

Realizing the Source and Purpose of Your Inner Path

"I feel very strongly that I am under the influence of things or questions which were left incomplete and unanswered by my parents and grandparents and more distant ancestors." – C. G. Jung (2009)

Jung stated that a person's inner path is seldom a simple reflection of external circumstances. It is shaped by deep, inherited layers of the psyche (Jung, 1960). The inner path appears to be connected to ancestral parts associated with family lineage (Hill, 2019). In his Red Book, Jung (2009) emphasized that these are not merely genetic traits, but dormant complexes, questions, and tendencies in the unconscious, waiting to shape our journey. He described ancestral imagos, their qualities, talents, and unresolved issues, as living forces within us (Jung, 1960a, para. 254). Inner peace comes from harmonizing these inner elements with our outer lives.

We have all met people who seem "predestined" for a mission, compelled by urgent ancestral questions left unanswered (Wolynn, 2016). Not everyone feels this drive so intensely, but these internal tendencies are within us all. Therapists routinely uncover echoes of past generations through dreamwork, imaginative dialogue, and journaling. This intuitive process is gaining support through neurobiological research on relational trauma, brain development, and neuroplasticity (Schore, 2001).

The path inward is rarely a direct map to outer achievements. Your inner path has a deeply significant, subtle influence on the friendships you form, the work you do, and the causes you are drawn to (Jung, 1963). Your inner path is a tapestry of family, culture, and humanity. I would humbly suggest that your ancestors lived very difficult lives and only the ones with a strong inner path succeeded in their family mission. Having an inner path is a human necessity that provides you with an intuitive sense of purpose. It is up to you to find and follow your inner path (Rohr, 2019).

A Lesson: Showing Me My Path

Here is a dialogue to help you find your path.
https://youtu.be/GXqrCk3f61U

1. Find a quiet space where you can relax and not be disturbed for at least 20 minutes.
2. Start with several cycles of relaxation, as described in Appendix A. Inhale for four counts, hold for four, exhale for four, hold for four. Allow your attention to drift inward, settling neatly into your body.
3. When you feel a sense of stillness, set a gentle intention: "I wish to see, hear, or sense what is true for me."
4. Now imagine yourself in a place that feels safe and open, such as a meadow, a quiet room, or an undefined place. Notice what is around you but do not force anything to appear. Just be present in the moment.
5. Make the invitation to your inner beloved: *I invite my inner guide, my innate wisdom and beloved presence, to appear and help me see my inner path.* Wait. Notice how this presence

manifests itself as a figure, a presence, a sense of warmth, a color, or simply a voice or intuition.

6. Notice what happens. Do images arise? Perhaps there is a river, a footpath, a mountain trail, or something more abstract that makes itself known to you. Do you feel drawn to certain directions in your mind's eye? What emotions, sensations, or words come up for you? Remind yourself that any response via images or subtle impressions has value. The answer may be so quietly whispered that you barely notice it.

7. Gently converse in your mind with whatever arises. Try to discover where the path leads. Notice any symbols so you can research them later for understanding. Ask questions: *What qualities do I need to walk on this path? Are there any companions for me on this path? How do I recognize this path in my outer life?*

8. Allow for responses and continue to listen and interact patiently. Notice if the answer is a feeling of ease, a new question, or even a loving silence. You might already be on your path and not even know it. Avoid steering the response with your own will. You are an objective observer in this process. Let your inner wisdom take the lead.

9. Close the session: Thank your inner beloved for their guidance, no matter how it was expressed. Slowly bring your attention back to the outer world with your breath and your eyes.

Any answer you get from inner dialogue will be in the form of symbols, stories, or emotions. Like dreams, they rarely make logical sense to the conscious ego, but if you sit with them for a while, they gain meaning through reflection. Don't hesitate to write or draw what you experienced. Make a record of your impressions and listen to them later to gain insight. Repeat this process regularly whenever you have a question or a followup. Similar to how water finds the lowest place, your path may reveal itself in subtle choices. This script is designed to honor the symbolic, intuitive wisdom of the psyche that guides you toward your unique journey. You will find an outer resonance that unfolds naturally as you live and reflect upon it.

Understanding the Spiritual Meaning of an Inner Path

"...the spiritual journey is about transformation, about allowing ourselves to be moved and changed by the Divine, to go beyond simply belonging to something." – Father Richard Rohr (2011, p. 30).

Religion is an emotionally charged word these days. Jung preferred the term personal spirituality because the dogma of cultural religion is often too rigid for people who seek their inner path (Jung, 1963). In the gospels, it is explained through metaphor that people should follow their inner path to truth. This has been interpreted as an invitation to inner transformation. We all start as babies in the crib, imbued with unconscious inner divinity. As we get older, we develop our ego, which begins our outward journey. If we also focus on our inner journey as adults, this leads us to a compassionate, authentic life of service, rather than a superficial following of strict, dogmatic rules (Rohr, 2019).

People turned the prophets into a religion of rules instead of a journey toward their union with God. This shift made religion all about "belonging and believing" instead of a spiritual journey of personal transformation (Rohr, 2019). Rather than faith, which relies on trust, I prefer a profound spiritual experience. Parishioners are merely inspired through faith. In my experience, clients are not just inspired but actually healed by having encounters with their own soul.

You are not called to be a prophet yourself, but instead to follow your own authentic path, just as they did. Find and follow your true path with a sense of self-awareness and courage to make a unique journey that is guided by your inner light. Shadows are made from light. But, just as surely as the day follows the night, we are merely human beings, with all the beauty and chaos that comes with the job. If you live in conversation with your inner beloved, you will be a better version of yourself.

You cannot find your inner path through your ego because it is blinded by the distractions of the material world. If you make the invitation, your inner beloved will seek you out. You can then ask your question and wait for guidance. When your inner beloved speaks to you, in its ancient way, listen and take careful note, with an attitude of awe and acceptance, to the power and wisdom of your inner beloved.

Distinguishing Inner Wealth Versus Ego Wealth

"Some people are so poor, all they have is money!" – Anonymous, commonly attributed to Bob Marley

The ego's pursuit of external goals is purely for survival's sake. Pursuing relationships, wealth, and social approval often lead to dissatisfaction if they are not aligned with the deeper needs of the soul (Jung, 1964; Stein, 1998). Without a deeper sense of connection to our inner beloved, people experience emptiness, lack of purpose, and a sense of spiritual death, regardless of their outward ego's success (Jung, 1966; Singer, 1994).

Depth psychologists encourage their clients to seek authenticity and inner wealth by engaging with their unconscious through dreams, active imagination, and any creative practice that allows messages to flow to and from their inner guide (Jung, 1966; Stein, 1998). Otherwise, clients are stuck in the ego-driven material world, with its depressing lack of meaning and authenticity. The process of gaining inner meaning helps clients integrate their unconscious material and develop a living relationship with their inner self. This brings a deeper sense of purpose and fulfillment that is lacking in external achievements alone (Jung, 1953; Stein, 1998).

There are deeper riches within the human soul than any material possessions can provide. Money and property can buy security, but not happiness. All the things that your culture tells you to acquire are devoid of meaning unless they hold a deeper significance within you. The riches of the soul are a way to avoid all the symptoms that outer dissatisfaction cannot solve.

A Lesson: What Is the Currency of Your Soul?

What does your soul consider wealth? It is unlikely to be material wealth, although it could be connected. For many people, inner wealth is family, connection, service, and friendship. For people who are driven to provide for their families, finding inner wealth is how they begin to acquire a peace of mind and a sense of direction that is not ruled by their bank balance or net worth. Y

You cannot enjoy your outer wealth if you have a deficit inside. https://youtu.be/CgP346cdX00

1. Find a comfortable, quiet place where you can relax and not be disturbed for at least 20 minutes.

2. Set an intention to be open to and receptive to whatever message or experience happens.

3. Enter your inner sanctuary. Close your eyes and imagine stepping into a safe, sacred inner space. A garden, temple, or welcoming place that makes you feel protected. Allow the details to emerge gradually. Relax.

4. Make a call to your inner beloved. Silently invite your inner wisdom to join you in this space in whatever form it chooses. Notice how this presence manifests itself, regardless of whether it is a person, symbol, feeling, voice, or just a presence.

5. Ask: *What is the currency of my soul?* Or ask: *What does true wealth mean to you, my inner beloved?* Allow the question to hang in the space. Let yourself feel the resonance and significance of the question.

6. Open yourself to a response. The inner self manifests differently for everyone. Notice what arises, whether it is a word, an image, an emotion, a sensation, or a feeling. Remain gently curious and do not judge the otherworldliness and symbolism of the inner response.

7. Deepen the experience with further dialogue, such as "How does my soul measure wealth? What is most precious and sustaining to you, my inner beloved?"

If you receive a response, gently explore it and note it for further research when you are fully awake, later. You might ask: *How can I cultivate this inner wealth in my daily life?*

If nothing comes, trust the process. Sometimes, the answer reveals itself later in stray thoughts, dreams, or startling coincidences.

8. Express gratitude to your inner beloved for their guidance, even if it was wordless or subtle. Slowly bring your awareness back to your breath, body, eyes, and the room.

9. Be sure to write, draw, or create anything that happened during the dialogue. There may be symbols, feelings, or messages. They may seem confusing or they may be like a story of fantasy. Revisit the question at different times. Answers may deepen and clarify the message through persistence, like when you refine a query.

Inner wealth comes in unexpected forms: love, connection, peace, integrity, honesty, courage, creativity, or authenticity. It is interesting to note that people often require inner wealth before they can gain outer wealth. This is like loving your inner self so that you can more fully love others.

Finding Inner Wealth

"People may spend their whole lives climbing the ladder of success only to find, once they reach the top, that the ladder is leaning against the wrong wall." – Thomas Merton (1961)

Our parents and our culture send us an unspoken message to "succeed." What that means varies from one person to another, but many people in the Western world seek material wealth. I am not denying that being rich solves a lot of problems. But this text is about finding what your soul wants, not about seeking what other people want you to find. If you are meant for wealth, it will find you. If your soul has other interests, you will surely fail as you struggle in vain to gain something that your soul doesn't care about.

Ask yourself why you are working so hard for material wealth? Try to understand who you are trying to please with all that work, those long hours, and the sacrifices you make in your personal life? Clients so often come to me without even realizing that they aren't living for themselves. What's worse is that they are usually living for someone or something else that doesn't even know or care.

Later on, there is a script dialogue that asks an important question: "Whose Life Are You Living?" So few people are actually living for themselves. A human being only gets a certain allotment of heartbeats in a lifetime. It seems like such a waste to spend your life meeting someone else's expectations. Most of us are called to fulfill the hopes and expectations of others, often at the cost of our own soul's quiet longings. This raises disturbing questions: If you are not living for yourself, are you taking care of yourself? Do you respect yourself? Are you taking responsibility for your own soul?

The price you pay for climbing the wrong mountain (or boarding the wrong train) gets higher and higher the farther you get from where your soul needs to be. Once you are living for yourself, you can begin finding the things that your inner beloved wants to give you: authenticity, awareness, connection, compassion for self and others.

The ego is terrible at seeking things because it sees what it wants to see instead of what is actually there. The soul sees inward toward the unique mission that you are here to accomplish. Your inner beloved will show you what really matters to you. Inner wealth is the state of your soul in relation to the things that matter deeply to you. What your ego has is rented for a short time. What your soul has spans the generations that come before and after you.

Ask yourself: "What are the relationships that matter to my inner beloved?" True inner wealth does something beautiful to you and the world around you. For many, a wealthy soul involves helping others or doing something useful for your community. What matters to you could be as simple as spending time with someone you care about or fixing something that is broken. These are activities for your soul. As a matter of priority, consider also the possibility of caring for and fixing yourself first.

Walking the Labyrinth with Your Soul

"May God stand between you and harm in all the empty places where you must walk." – The Egyptian Book of the Dead (1885/1500 BCE)

Finding your inner path is about finding the riches in your soul. On this path, you will find art, beauty, and nature. On this journey, you will learn to touch and commune with your unconscious inner self. Instead of seeking things obsessively, stay open and find the things that your soul draws you to. Ask your inner beloved to help you find your path.

Inside of you is an inner labyrinth that represents the inner path you should be following. The guidance you receive will come from messages via dreams, imaginings, and creative work. Art, beauty, and nature surrounds your path. Your path includes your body, which also needs care. You need to find your authentic path. No one can find it for you, although many can help point the way.

If you find yourself stuck in a circle rather than a spiral, endlessly repeating the path already traveled, try something new. Break a habit. Have an inner conversation and learn how to get unstuck so that you can find the way to your inner path.

I drove through the desert, knowing that my old car was probably going to break down and leave us stranded, with no way to communicate our emergency. My inner beloved came to me, in my ego's time of fear, and held me close. "You have no need to fear. I will hold you. I will protect you. Do not ask how I do this, because you are unaware of the powers that I have." I smiled to myself and felt a sense of relief wash over me like holy water poured from an ancient urn. Now I knew that we would be okay. And we were. The next day, when the time was right, the car broke down where we could be saved.

You cannot call such things miracles, because the impossible is, by definition, not allowed in the physical world. But it felt like that old Egyptian blessing. This incredible thing happened, and I felt touched by the unconscious and enlightened. There are greater things in my life than I can understand.

Later, when our poor old car was replaced, I felt called to drive over to my old church. From my previous visits, I knew that one parishioner had set up a labyrinth years ago. As I sat in the church parking lot, my inner beloved asked me to walk with him in the labyrinth. I entered through the middle path, because I prefer the balance of being in the center in both mind, body, and spirit. I walked the path with my hands in my pockets, looking down and ahead at the turning path in front of me. I thought about the long path I had travelled in my life, and I heard the voice of my inner beloved, thanking me for coming here to walk with him. Tears sprang to my eyes with the knowledge that he was with me. I thanked my inner beloved humbly for saving me earlier, when I was in peril on the road. He smiled and said that we had both saved each other many times on the road that we have travelled together.

    After the walk, as I was leaving, I noticed some glass beads, and I picked up four of them and walked over to one of the benches nearby. I said four prayers, one for each bead, and, one-by-one, dropped each bead next to the bench. Each bead landed on a pile of other glass beads. So I knew that others had come before me and said similar prayers after walking the labyrinth.

Photograph © 2023 Scott Hensley, used with permission 2025

Later, I thanked the person who helped design and build the church's labyrinth. I am grateful when I meet people who understand the power and the glory of symbolism made manifest in soulful places on this Earth. Sacred places are not always in the sanctuaries, but often in the gardens nearby. Not always is holiness in the beautiful places, but sometimes the soul is found in the deserts and other forgotten places. May you find your own sacred place somewhere on the path of your life's journey.

References

Budge, E. A. Wallis (Trans.). (1895). *The Egyptian Book of the Dead*. Dover Publications. (Original work published c. 1500 BCE)

Hensley, S. (2023). *Labyrinth at St. James the Apostle Episcopal Church* [Photograph]. Labyrinth Locator. https://labyrinthlocator.org/labyrinth/saint-james-the-apostle-episcopal-church/344/

Hill, K. (2019). *Unveiling the Self: How Jungian Therapy Helps with Identity and Purpose*. Retrieved December 1, 2025, from https://www.kevinwgrant.com/blog/item/unveiling-the-self

Jung, C. G. (1953). *Two essays on analytical psychology* (R. F. C. Hull, Trans., Vol. 7, Collected Works). Princeton University Press.

Jung, C. G. (1960). *The structure and dynamics of the psyche*. In *The collected works of C. G. Jung* (R. F. C. Hull, Trans.; Vol. 8). Princeton University Press.

Jung, C. G. (1963). *Memories, dreams, reflections* (A. Jaffé, Ed.; R. & C. Winston, Trans.). Pantheon Books.

Jung, C. G. (1964). *Man and his symbols* (R. F. C. Hull, Trans.). Dell Publishing. (Original anthology published 1961)

Jung, C. G. (2009). *The Red Book: Liber Novus* (S. Shamdasani, Ed. & Trans.). W. W. Norton & Company. (Original work published circa 1914–1930)

Lao Tzu. (1997). *Lao Tzu: Tao te ching – A book about the way and the power of the way* (U. K. Le Guin, Trans.). Shambhala.

Merton, T. (1961). *New seeds of contemplation*. New Directions Publishing.

Rohr, R. (2011). *Falling upward: A spirituality for the two halves of life*. Jossey-Bass.

Rohr, R. (2019). *The Universal Christ: How a Forgotten Reality Can Change Everything We See, Hope for, and Believe.* Convergent Books.

Schore, A. N. (2001). The effects of early relational trauma on right brain development, affect regulation, and infant mental health. *Infant Mental Health Journal*, 22(1-2), 201–269. https://www.allanschore.com/pdf/SchoreIMHJTrauma01.pdf

Singer, T. (1994). *Boundaries of the soul: The practice of Jung's psychology.* Anchor Books.

Stein, M. (1998). *Jung's map of the soul: An introduction.* Open Court.

Wolynn, M. (2016). *It didn't start with you: How inherited family trauma shapes who we are and how to end the cycle.* Penguin Books. (See www.redbeardsomatictherapy.com/post/the-ghosts-of-our-ancestors-how-intergenerational-trauma-shapes-our-genes for practical clinical examples)

6 Finding Your Calling

> *"What did you do as a child that made the hours pass like minutes? Herein lies the keys to your earthly pursuits."* – Anonymous, but commonly attributed to C. G. Jung

There is an old saying: lend your abilities to your work and your talents to your soul. Few are lucky enough to make a living with their soul-given talent. It is difficult to find a deeply meaningful job that can sustain you. If you find something that you love doing while making money at it, you should do it.

For everyone else who cannot "follow their bliss" at work, the solution is to be in service to whatever job you can find. Before you can be in service to others, however, you need to make sure you are living and working in service of yourself.

A Lesson: Whose Life Are You Living?

If you are on your own path, you cannot expect to live up to anyone else's expectations except your own. Earlier, you did the script that revealed what you are carrying. There is a larger question, however. Who are you carrying it for? This brings up the question of who are you actually living for?

This seems like an odd question, but it turns out that most people are doing things to please those around them. Most people are living to satisfy the demands and expectations of their family, society, or their peer group (Spielman et al., 2020). It is difficult to live an authentic life that is not of their own choosing. Many people are miserable when they are unconsciously living to fulfill the expectations of others.

You cannot be on an authentic journey if you aren't living for yourself. https://youtu.be/thZ2vbTFnVY

1. Settle in. Find a quiet space, close your eyes, lie or sit, and do some relaxed breathing: four counts in through the nose, four counts holding, and four counts out through the mouth until your whole body is relaxed. Invite a sense of curiosity and compassion into your creative space.

2. Summon the doer who is living your life.

There is a part of me that is busy living life in a certain way. I invite that part of me to step forward.

3. Notice what comes up. It may be a symbol, a feeling, an image. Is it an achiever? Is it a rebel? Is it an obedient son or daughter?

4. Greet the doer and thank them for coming. Tell them you want to understand them better.

What am I hoping to achieve by living this way? What values or standards am I trying to meet?

5. Explore the sources and influences of the doer. Invite the doer part to show or tell.

Whose voice do you listen to when making choices? Is it a parent, a teacher, peers, community, or society?

6. Gently ask about authenticity.

How do you feel about the life I am living now? Does it feel true to our inner beloved, or more like a performance meant to please someone else?

7. Perhaps the doer will show you the answer, or introduce you to some other inner part that represents what you really want to do.

8. Ask the doer if they will step back so you can meet the part of you who knows what your soul truly wants.

Can I speak to the part of me that carries the desires and yearnings of my soul?

9. What comes up for you? Perhaps it will be a stray thought of an image of your inner child, playing or doing something that you really love to do.

10. Hold a dialogue with the part that represents what you really want to do and who you really want to be. Here are some powerful questions to ask your soulful self:

Whose life are we living, really? Who gets to decide what matters most to us?

11. Affirm your intention to live authentically by saying something like this:

I know there are many expectations and influences shaping my choices. I honor those, but I need to live for myself. I am giving myself permission to live more authentically, for the sake of my soul. I need to live from the inside out, not from the outside in.

12. Continue to have these dialogues as long as they seem useful. Eventually, quicken your breath, open your eyes, and welcome yourself back.

The goal of this script is not to criticize parts that crave approval or safety, but to listen with compassion and understand which influences are aligned with your true self. Some people really should live for others, but others have a higher responsibility to themselves. By using gentle curiosity, your inquiry can reveal deep-seated patterns and open up a pathway toward living an authentic, soulful life.

Lending Your Abilities to Your Work and Your Talents to Your Soul

It can be a real shock to some of my Western clients when we discover together, through inner conversation, that they are not living for themselves. Clients in Asian societies are often less surprised because they are expected to owe a duty to family and community in more collectivist cultures (Kuo & Roysircar, 2004).

Humans in most cultures find it difficult to do work that is the calling of their heart. Mark and Pearson (2001) explain that the caregiver archetype prioritizes care and service to family and community first over the needs of the individual. The health of the tribe's soul was assigned to shamans in ancient societies, while most members of the tribe focused on family and clan survival (Eliade, 1964).

Duty to family and community first is still true in modern life, where less than two percent of the workforce actually make a living as a professional creative person (Americans for the Arts, 2023; U.S. Bureau of Labor Statistics, 2025). Those who aren't in that two percent must make compromises to serve the needs of our families. The younger generations, who are sometimes less willing to compromise, face difficulties supporting a family or securing a retirement (Benefit News, 2023; NIH, 2013). Despite these criticisms, I uspect that the younger generations may be correct.

Employers' use of mechanization and artificial intelligence is forcing people away from fields where computers excel, and toward human abilities and talents that software cannot do well. This does not change the fact that most people's creative talents are not enough to make a living wage (Agrawal et al., 2018). The rest of us will still need to compromise in finding work that sustains our families. This will involve doing something that is not what our inner beloved would choose.

The great mistake that most people make is being unwilling to compromise their principles. The older generations often abandon their creative hobbies in favor of profit. Whereas the younger generations are sometimes more willing to live in idealistic poverty, waiting for their big break as professional artists. Jung (1966/1971) viewed creativity as vital to our health, but warned against over identifying with it too much (dissociation). The Buddhists suggest a middle way, where family obligations are integrated with creativity to foster wholeness without taking extreme measures (Edinger, 1985; Stein, 2019).

Realizing Creativity Is Not All-Or-Nothing

Being a professional artist does not require giving up a living wage, and being a professional capitalist does not require selling your soul to the corporation. Creative fulfillment can live in everyday moments and small practices, such as writing poetry before going to bed, working on weekend projects, tending a small garden, doing charity work that helps others, or building a playground in the backyard. The joy of creativity is present whether or not you monetize it (Csikszentmihalyi, 1996; Wrzesniewski & Dutton, 2001).

There is a time to reap and a time to sow, as the Bible so wisely states in Ecclesiastes 3:1-2. If you are called to support your partner and children, creative pursuits may shrink or morph into "fun time with the kids" while they are young. Family obligations should not, however, allow creativity and beauty to vanish. Quite the contrary, raising children is an opportunity for parens to get back in touch with their inner child. The balance will shift back to adult creativity when circumstances change.

Living a hybrid creative life does not represent artistic failure. If you are "moonlighting" as an artist on the side while providing for your family, this is success. Many renowned artists held other jobs throughout their lives to maintain a standard of living. The key idea is to avoid equating material success with artistic worth. You should not judge a practical job as a betrayal of your inner muse.

Thankless jobs and careers can sometimes turn into creative opportunities if you keep in touch with your inner beloved and stay self-aware. It is not uncommon to suddenly "find" an opportunity at work that takes advantage of your creative skills.

Early careers and jobs are often uncreative and boring until you have mastered the skills. Think of your early job as an apprenticeship. It takes countless hours to fine-tune your craft with disciplined practice and soulful dedication. Work seems like drudgery, but the soul loves to work in the low places on the fine details. As your skills improve, you find, almost as if by magic, you are using nearly all of your creative skills to do the work. This happens when you reach the level of a "master" in your craft. This is when your inner beloved becomes involved, because your work is now as much an art as it is a science.

You should keep your personal creativity alive for the sake of your soul. Wise people spend their lives quietly and joyfully practicing their creative arts without the thought of money or notoriety, or perhaps in spite of it.

Listen to your inner beloved. Each person's balance of creativity and practicality is unique. Some people need more security, while others are driven to actively pursue risky creativity. Listen with honesty and patience to that quiet voice inside you and adapt your life as needed when it calls to you. My creativity started with writing music and playing it on the piano. Eventually, I wrote music and lyrics for a performance that was staged at the Hoogland Theater in Springfield, Illinois. Just recently, I wrote this book. It wasn't about the money, because there wasn't hardly any. Each act of creativity was about the story that my soul needed to tell at the time. I encourage you to let your inner beloved tell your story: whether anyone else ever hears it or not is irrelevant, because you are the one who needs it most of all.

I encourage you to be a servant to your life and your work, whatever it may be. Being in service to your soul is the wisest way to stay flexible and available so that you can find your calling.

Bringing Soul into the Workplace

Hollis (1998) has noted that the collective soul rarely inhabits the workplace. Most capitalist corporations lack soul because their purpose is to attain wealth by compensating their employees for their productivity. Rare is the company who nurtures their employees like a parent (Hollis, 1998).

Companies usually reflect the neurotic weaknesses of their executives. An organization's behavior usually mirrors the needs and shadows of their leaders. An employee cannot reasonably expect this behavior to change if the same imperfect executives are still in charge. It is smarter and more realistic to simply seek employment elsewhere (Hollis, 1998).

The best executives and managers, however, realize that their own survival depends, to a certain extent, on the well-being of their employees. Wise employees will seek organizations with strong personnel departments and confidential Employee Assistance programs that can help them in times of need. Beware of companies that use organizational psychology (OP) to study productive behavior. OP is usually focused on efficiency and productivity, not matters of the individual soul (Hollis, 1998; Mirvis, 1997).

Companies that authentically take suggestions from their employees are often the best places to work (Hollis, 1998; Mirvis, 1997). Starbucks and Microsoft are good examples, overall, of employers that maintain high profit margins while providing employees with comprehensive health benefits, mental health care, employee assistance, family support, educational subsidies, and other well-being perks.

A less common but even more effective way to run a company is to hire managers and directors who can address the soulful needs of their employees. I have noticed that this usually works best by promoting long-term employees who are in touch with the heart and soul of the company. Soulful managers can often balance the corporate need for profits with the soulful needs of the workers who are paid to make that happen. Hollis (1998) notes that a therapist can only take a client as far as their own personal development. Likewise, I have noticed that departments can only progress as far as their managers have in matters of their wisdom and soul. Hiring soulful managers is an enlightened way to improve morale and increase retention. Soulful leadership invites healing and compassion into the workplace.

The best way to achieve positive energy in a corporate environment is through humble service with no expectation of soulful benefit. You can do this through a concept called *servant leadership* (Greenleaf, 1970).

Practicing Servant Leadership

Service is like tending to your inner garden. Being in service to yourself and others tends to yours and others' souls. You can serve your family with a paycheck. You can serve your colleagues with your efforts. You can serve your wider community with your attitude, regardless of what you do or the environment you do it in (Greenleaf, 1970).

You don't need to be a manager or an owner to practice servant leadership. Servant leadership is a mindset, not a title. Servant leadership is a perspective on life where you focus on helping those around you grow and succeed. Being a servant in your work draws on a deep inner commitment to serve others and the organization with honesty and care. Whether those you serve return the favor is irrelevant. If you think of yourself as "being in service" to both your inner beloved and your work, you cannot put your foot wrong (Greenleaf, 1977).

When you are "in service to others," you practice deep listening and focus on understanding the perspectives of those around you. You are present and attentive to their needs. You support and validate people and vice versa, even if you cannot help them. You support people's growth and encourage their strengths and talents by offering your help, your time, and your words of encouragement. You mentor those around you by sharing your knowledge with no expectation of reward. You are not selling a service; you are providing a service. You facilitate teamwork by including others and creating space for quieter voices. The best servants are models for ethical behavior, integrity, and humility. Great servants work hard and ask for nothing in return. Servants lead by example, regardless of their actual position in the hierarchy. A servant to others exemplifies their strength of character and inspires others to do the same (Greenleaf, 1977).

Being in service to others is not about submissiveness or sacrificing your health, but it can be exhausting. Effective servant leaders take care of their bodies and souls by resting. While you are serving others, be sure to maintain your own well-being and boundaries. Anyone, a client, counselor, or co-worker, can practice being supportive, compassionate, and collaborative. When you serve others, you subtly influence those around you and the wider culture at large by inspiring them. In many ways, a servant is actually a master who leads informally (Greenleaf, 1977).

Servant leaders in various cultures are teachers, gurus, shamans, priests, and soul guides. They serve as healers and mentors within their communities, embodying what some traditions call dharma, which is a sacred duty to live in harmony and serve others. With dharma, the leader accepts ethical and spiritual responsibility for the welfare of all. In many cultures, service is a universal responsibility; even the CEO of the company serves others because their success is everyone's success. A shaman in Indigenous cultures serves as the community healer and spiritual guide. In South Asian cultures, a guru is a spiritual teacher who leads by example, dedicated to fostering the growth of others (Russell & Stone, 2002; Eva et al., 2019).

From a global perspective, servant leadership is a way of influencing and supporting others that transcends job titles and formal authority. Not surprisingly, many people who are good servant leaders find themselves put in positions of leadership eventually because the greatest leaders tend to embody servant leadership principles. Abraham Lincoln was Dale Carnegie's (1936) model for how to be an outstanding leader. There is a lot of overlap between Carnegie's training institute and the leadership style that Lincoln exemplified: humility, empathy, appreciation, communication, collaboration, and putting others first before yourself. The greatest leaders conduct themselves as servants to the rest of humanity. In service, they lead, and in leading, they serve.

Finding a Soulful Vocation

"If the path before you is clear, you're probably on someone else's". –Anonymous, but commonly attributed to Joseph Campbell

One of the most difficult things you can do is to find something that sustains you and moves you forward in your body and soul. It is important not to walk in someone else's path. Do your own thing. Be selfish and don't apologize for it. Keep your distance from people who judge you harshly for doing what your heart desires. This advice comes from my western sensibility. If I were to rewrite this for eastern ears, it would be different.

For the Eastern mind, the path is not carved by one's will alone, but revealed through harmony with the greater whole. To follow your heart is not rebellion, but alignment. The small self moves in rhythm with the larger flow of life. In this way, selfishness becomes sincerity: a quiet honoring of one's true place within your authentic way of being. The task is not to separate from others but to remain centered among them, like the still point at the heart of a turning world.

Most people do not know what they should do to sustain themselves, heart and soul. This is easily solved by traveling and experimenting. Whether or not you pass all your exams, traveling outside your birthplace is the best way to learn how other people live and love. Discovering other cultures, other family structures, religions, and economies gives you a healthy perspective on your own.

When you are trying to discover what you should do, trying new things is a good idea, especially while you are young and unencumbered by family obligations. Enroll in a school far from home and study unusual things that call to you from within. Socialize with people who do things differently. Ask people to let you observe them at work to see what the job is really like, as opposed to your own preconceptions of the work.

During your travels and experiments, you will probably discover how terrible the corporate shadow is. Try not to be discouraged. The workplace is filled with shadow, but it is also filled with important life lessons. If you can survive in the workplace, you can survive anywhere, even in your family shadow. Be ready and willing to walk through the fire of initiation into the work that represents your life's journey. The soul needs initiation, and the workplace will demand your sacrifice.

Lastly, do not assume that you have to do something just because your friends say you do. Don't follow the money or the prestige. So many people settle for a degree in a popular field of study just because their parents want them to. Instead, follow your instincts, because when a job appeals to your heart and soul, you are less likely to be discouraged.

Walking Joyfully Through the Fire

"The difference between a good life and a bad life is how well you walk through the fire." – Anonymous, commonly attributed to C. G. Jung

You can effectively manage your life by staying calmly positive and encouraging others and yourself to take responsibility. Approaching life-management from a place of anxious worry and sleepless torment rarely works. The wise person embodies stillness and centered calmness. One speaks sparingly but with certainty. Before asking a question, you should already have an answer in mind, but remain open to learning something new, and always be willing to change your mind.

You should allow people the freedom and space for creativity and fresh perspective. People hate change because they do not realize how beautiful a new opportunity is. You can be their guide. Stay positive and lead people towards change by letting them pick the path that works best for them, not you. Once they are on the path, smile and give them a wave as they forge into the future.

Openness and acceptance is the way to walk, unaffected, through the fires of chaos. As Kipling (1910) says, you must keep your head when all around you are losing theirs. Thus, you can walk joyfully, hand-in-hand with your inner beloved, through the madness that life inevitably throws at you.

References

Agrawal, A., Gans, J., & Goldfarb, A. (2018). *Prediction machines: The simple economics of artificial intelligence*. Harvard Business Review Press.

Americans for the Arts. (2023). *Creative industries research and data*. https://www.americansforthearts.org/by-program/reports-and-data/research-studies-publications/creative-industries

Barrett, L. (2022). *A Jungian approach to coaching: The theory and practice of turning leaders into people*. Routledge.

Behson, S. J. (2013). Generational differences in work-family conflict and synergy. *Journal of Occupational and Organizational Psychology*, 86(1), 1–23. https://doi.org/10.1111/joop.12000

Benefit News. (2023, November 7). *25% of Gen Z workers are supporting their parents, study finds*. https://www.benefitnews.com/news/25-of-gen-z-workers-are-supporting-their-parents-study-finds

Carnegie, D. (1936). *How to win friends and influence people*. New York, NY: Simon & Schuster.

Csikszentmihalyi, M. (1996). *Creativity: Flow and the psychology of discovery and invention*. Harper Perennial.

Edinger, E. F. (1985). *Ego and archetype: Individuation and the religious function of the psyche*. Shambhala.

Eliade, M. (1964). *Shamanism: Archaic techniques of ecstasy*. Princeton University Press.

Finkelstein, G., Harris, K., & Shen, J. (2017). Servant leadership in nonprofit culture. *USF Blogs*.

Greenleaf, R. K. (1970). *The servant as leader*. Robert K. Greenleaf Center.

Greenleaf, R. K. (1977). *Servant leadership: A journey into the nature of legitimate power and greatness*. Paulist Press.

Hollis, J. (1998). *The Eden project: In search of the magical other*. Inner City Books.

Hollis, J. (2001). *Creating a life: Finding your individual path*. Inner City Books.

Jung, C. G. (1968). *The archetypes and the collective unconscious* (R. F. C. Hull, Trans.). In H. Read, M. Fordham, & G. Adler (Eds.), The collected works of C. G. Jung: Vol. 9, Part 1 (pp. 3-41). Princeton University Press. (Original work published 1959).

Jung, C. G. (1971). *Psychological types* (H. G. Baynes, Trans.). Princeton University Press. (Original work published 1921).

Kipling, R. (1910). If—. In *Rewards and Fairies*. London, England: Macmillan.

Kuo, B. C. H., & Roysircar, G. (2004). Infusing collectivism into counseling: A cultural formulation. *The Counseling Psychologist*, 32(1), 159–165. https://doi.org/10.1177/0011000003261214.

Mark, M., & Pearson, C. S. (2001). *The hero and the outlaw: Building extraordinary brands through the power of archetypes*. McGraw-Hill.

Mirvis, P. H. (1997). "Soul work" in organizations. *Organization Science*, 8(2), 193–215. https://doi.org/10.1287/orsc.8.2.192

Russell, R. F., & Stone, A. G. (2002). A review of servant leadership attributes: Developing a practical model. *Leadership & Organization Development Journal*, 23(3), 145-157. https://doi.org/10.1108/01437730210424

Spielman, R. M., Jenkins, W. J., & Lovett, M. D. (2020). *The many varieties of conformity. In Principles of social psychology*. BCcampus. https://pressbooks.bccampus.ca/socialpsychben/.

Stein, M. (Ed.). (1992). *Psyche at work: Workplace applications of Jungian analytical psychology*. Chiron Publications.

Stein, M. (2019). *Individuation*. Chiron Publications.

U.S. Bureau of Labor Statistics. (2025). *Arts and design occupations*. https://www.bls.gov/ooh/arts-and-design/

United Nations Conference on Trade and Development. (2021). *Creative economy outlook 2021*. https://unctad.org/publication/creative-economy-outlook-2021

Wrzesniewski, A., & Dutton, J. E. (2001). Crafting a job: Revisioning employees as active crafters of their work. *Academy of Management Review*, 26(2), 179-201. https://doi.org/10.5465/amr.2001.4378011

7 Finding Good Relationships

"To love is to find yourself in the other, not to possess or control, but to discover a dimension of yourself in union with another. True partnership grows quietly when two people let themselves be found rather than trying to force a connection through will or desire." – Robert A. Johnson (1986, p. 74)

Finding good relationships is probably the hardest thing most people ever do. It certainly was for me. It is unnecessary to have a great relationship with your inner beloved in order to have successful relationships, but it sure helps. More important than your relationship with your inner beloved, though, is whether you like yourself.

People who have a poor view of themselves tend to have bad relationships that mirror what they think of themselves. If you don't think you deserve happiness, you often get involved with people who make you unhappy.

People seek relationships based on whatever trauma and damage has been done to them. This is why the ego is so terrible at finding intimate partners. People are blind when it comes to finding good relationships because they see what they want to see instead of what is actually in front of their eyes.

This is why the secret to a successful relationship is to let your soul find it, as Johnson (1986) suggests. Discovering a relationship rather than forcing the issue works much better.

You kind of "get what you give" in relationships. Your inner beloved is a guide who can show you how to be a friend to yourself. Once you know how to treat yourself well, it is easier to be a friend to others.

A Lesson: Being a Friend to Yourself

The art of self-care is, literally, being a genuine friend to yourself as if you were another person. Being nice to yourself is both an art and a responsibility to yourself and those around you.

Work through the dialogue in your own time, compassionately, and find your way towards being an honest friend to yourself. https://youtu.be/MmhwkOnSGRc

1. Sit or lie comfortably. Close your eyes or soften your gaze. Take a few slow, deep breaths. There are some nice relaxation techniques in Appendix A if you need them.

2. In your mind's eye, picture yourself in a place where you feel safe and accepted. There are two empty chairs facing each other. One chair is for your inner beloved, and the other is for you, the observing self.

Your observer self is not your ego per se, but an active observer version of yourself who is neutral but participating, listening, and learning. This is the same observer that watches your dreams on the stage of your inner mind's eye. But you are awake now, so you can remember this easier.

3. Find a creative way to invite your inner beloved to take the other chair. For me, my inner beloved is always changing in every encounter. Perhaps this time he or she is an image, a shadow, a quiet feeling, a symbol, an invisible presence, and so forth.

4. Have a gentle but honest conversation about being a better friend to yourself. Your observer self can ask things like:

What is it like for you, being within me, day after day?

Are there ways you wish I treated you differently, as a friend would?

What do you need from me that I never give to you?

How can we be more compassionate and caring toward each other?

The idea behind being compassionate and caring toward yourself is that most people are very hard on themselves and expect perfection. Think about ways you can be nicer to yourself. Think about ways that your inner beloved can treat you better and vice versa. Remember that your inner beloved is not perfect either. Talk about this.

Caring for your soul is the goal here. As you gain acceptance of yourself, you become more flexible and forgiving toward yourself and others. This can be a painful process, but over time it gets easier to see yourself clearly and accept it.

5. Now imagine switching seats. Take the seat of your inner beloved and have him/her sit in your seat. Now your roles are reversed. Try to see yourself as your inner beloved sees you. Invite your inner beloved to show you how he/she sees you.

If I could do one thing for you, it would be...

When you are struggling, I wish that you would remember to...

6. Return to your seat as the observer after absorbing the other one's perspective. Take a moment to thank your inner friend for being honest and for participating. As you leave the imaginary place, consider this: what new gestures could you treat yourself to with friendship in daily life, big or small? Perhaps you could get yourself a carton of ice cream as a reward for doing something difficult today.

7. After you open your eyes, notice your breathing and your body. Be sure to make a record of your reflections before you forget them. What surprised you about your inner friend's responses? In what situations do you notice yourself turning against yourself and your own self-interests or happiness? How

can you practice being a friend to yourself, especially when you feel challenged, lonely, or triggered? How can you care for yourself when you are forcing yourself to "tough it out?" How can you be a friend to yourself, not just on the inside, but in the outside world?

This script is intentionally gentle and relational, but works better with self-honesty. Writing afterwards in a journal is often a wonderful way to help you see, in words, how your inner beloved sees you.

Inner friendship scripts help people make contact with internal experiences in language that build trust and respect between aspects of themselves. This is crucial for healing emotional divides and giving you experience with self-compassion (Schwartz, 1995). We could all be better, more satisfied people if we were more compassionate with ourselves and others (Kimmel, 2012; Bly, 1990; Woodman, 1980).

Knowing Yourself Through Others

"Oh would some Power give us the gift
To see ourselves as others see us!
It would from many blunders free us,
And foolish notion:
What airs in dress and gait would leave us,
And even devotion!." – Robert Burns (1786)

Having an objective, accurate picture of yourself is almost impossible. The mind protects itself from the painful truth of who we actually are. Learning the truth is difficult, but it can be done in two ways. I mentioned earlier that you can take a personality test and learn about your "tendencies." Tests are not personal, though, so you won't learn anything surprising. A better way to know yourself is through a consensus of what other people think of you. Especially people who either know you very well or who don't know you at all. They won't tell you directly, of course. You need to find clever ways of learning what other people say behind your back.

The best way I've found to understand myself through others is to cultivate a set of very honest, blunt friends and family members whom I can trust to tell me the truth. It also helps to make fun of yourself sometimes and watch carefully for a reaction. If you hit the mark, people will laugh and tease you. As this process continues, you gradually build up a picture of what other people think of you. It won't be 100% accurate, but you will learn some fairly accurate things about yourself that are both pleasant and unpleasant. If you see something that you really don't like, you can make adjustments. Or you can just learn to accept that part of yourself, as-is, and laugh along with everyone else.

A friend of mine and I were talking about her husband, and I mentioned how much I appreciate his thoughtfulness and sense of humor. She didn't recognize my description of her spouse. "That's nice, but I never see that side of him." That's a fairly typical reaction. She's too close to recognize her husband's nice attributes (unless it's all an act). As with most spouses, she only sees the things that irritate her.

The same idea applies to knowing yourself. You are too close to be objective. It is so difficult to discover and admit bad things that you dislike about yourself. It is easier to project those unappealing things onto other people and judge them, mercilessly. Following your authentic inner path is difficult, though, if you don't know who you actually are.

My friend Jane is basically her grandmother, and she knows it. She is a seeker of truth, and surrounds herself with an exclusive set of very trusted, very honest friends. When she bakes bread or makes matzo balls, they tease her about how she is just like her grandmother. She smiles, nods, and wonders how else she is like her Bubbe. It turns out that most people are similar to other people they knew when they were children, for better and for worse.

Finding Relationships Vs. Seeking Them

In relationships, the inner beloved is often confused with or projected onto your intimate partner (Hollis, 1993). It is important to avoid falling in love with an image of yourself that is not really them. This can happen to nearly anyone. People are well known for falling hopelessly in love with some lovely individual, only to divorce them a few years later when they realize that they are not at all who they thought they were. Sometimes people fall in love with someone imperfect who can, perhaps, protect them from a chaotic world. They think that the imperfections of the protector can be changed later. But this is an illusion: no one can change another person.

There are all kinds of mistakes that you might make when you fall in love: idealizing or ignoring your partner's flaws, expecting perfection, and projecting your issues onto them rather than taking responsibility for your own dark aspects. Being blind to your partner's true humanity can prevent the spiritual growth necessary for a healthy partnership (Hillman, 1975).

Being self-aware was probably my first step towards avoiding those kinds of mistakes. The minute I noticed myself falling in love with my future wife, I began making notes in my diary to help prevent myself from falling into these common traps. I felt it was important for me to see my fiance as an actual partner and an individual, not some inner vision that doesn't exist.

Ever since we moved in together, I have worked with my inner beloved to accept my shadow so that I don't project it onto her. I try to identify and own my own feelings to avoid blaming her. Best as I can, I try to take responsibility for myself and my actions. I know I am not perfect, so I try hard to work collaboratively with her to resolve any disputes. I'm not afraid to say I'm sorry, nor am I afraid to stand my ground when I am not the problem.

It is better, by far, to find your partner as an extension of who you are and the path you are walking on with your inner beloved. Instead of searching frantically, as the ego often does, just relax and find your partner in the places where you and your soul like to walk. If you love to read, perhaps you will find them by sharing an interest in books. If you love to hike, then perhaps you will find them on the trail leading towards your future. Not everyone finds a life partner, of course, but you always have your inner beloved, and hopefully also your close friends and family. If you spend your life open and self-aware, you will find something that will resound with your inner beloved.

Finding a relationship is far better than forcing one through instinctive behavior. If there is friendship and mutual interest, there is the possibility of intimacy and inner meaning (Johnson, 1986).

Finding Mystical Companionship

A relationship with your inner beloved might be surpassed sometimes by what I like to call a mystical companionship, which is a step beyond love that involves the great love of your life. Companionship extends your state of being into the shared presence of another. This is not a relationship of doing but of being together. There is acceptance and mutual recognition. Companionship flourishes and nourishes a fundamental human need to experience connection that transcends verbal exchange and task-driven interaction, a theme echoed by archetypal and soul-oriented writers (Hillman, 1975; Johnson, 1986; Moore, 1992).

This may not be a physical relationship. It may involve a "great other" presence in your life that offers a transcendent relationship. This may be a lifelong friend, partner, spiritual or natural force, or even a higher calling (Moore, 1992). Jack London was called to the wild. Shakespeare had a literary relationship with the "fair youth." Teresa of Avila had a mystical relationship with John of the Cross. Mary, the mother of Jesus, had a visitation with her cousin, Elizabeth, as described in the Gospel of Luke. My close relationship with my wife evolved over time to where we are now companions in life. A similar but unmarried variation of a mystical companion could be Abraham Lincoln's relationship with Joshua Speed.

This kind of companionship is metaphysical and may involve Jung's concept of the Self or some aspect of the inner beloved. The great other companion reflects your own depths and offers space for growth, acknowledgement, and balance. It is a sacred presence that is a gift (Hillman, 1975; Johnson, 1986; Moore, 1992).

Companionship supports intuitive, emotional aspects of the psyche by providing a safe and nurturing area for vulnerabilities to emerge, be held, and healed. Contrast that with the modern concept of a cultural or personal relationship that is merely physical and public. In a spiritual companionship, the individual does not prove or perform anything, but simply exists and is witnessed (Hillman, 1975; Johnson, 1986; Moore, 1992).

Companionship enriches life by bridging the inner world and the outer world, honoring the mystery of human connection, and inviting you into a deeper experience of presence, love, and belonging (Hillman, 1975; Johnson, 1986; Moore, 1992).

Caring For Your Soul

Taking care of your soul is how you tend to the relationship you have with yourself. Soul care is a sacred dialogue between you and your inner beloved. Tending to your soul means cultivating that partnership. If you make a daily invitation to ritual, imagination, and compassionate listening, this allows you to nurture depth, presence, and meaning along your life's journey (Moore, 1992; Schwartz, 1995; Holmes, 2022). But what is the soul?

Moore (1992) and others define the soul as a *numinous* or ethereal part of the human psyche that guides and teaches. The soul comes to people in their dreams and imaginings. It contains shadows of discarded parts of them, like the personal shadow, but it also contains older parts of their unconscious that they have never seen. If people care for their souls, their souls will take care of them too.

Care not cure. The focus of soul care is not in fixing impossible problems, but in listening to your soul's needs. Do not banish difficult feelings and symptoms, but instead invite them into a discussion (Moore, 1992).

Soul depth. The soul is not so much a thing as a deep experience, like a presence in your creative imagination. You can find sacred meaning in ordinary acts and daily routines (Moore, 1992). Humans have been doing simple, soulful things since the beginning of time: gardening, walking in nature, sewing, or creating something beautiful or meaningful.

Embrace complexity. Taking care of your soul means honoring life's contradictions. Joy follows suffering, light follows shadow, and dependence follows independence. You will need to expand your awareness of life's many complicated faces. Tend to your inner relationship. The many parts and characters within you make up who you actually are. Being in a relationship with your inner self is a partnership and an ongoing dialogue (Moore, 1992; Schwartz, 1995).

Active imagination. It is important to invite a dialogue with your soul to guide your ego. This process is a powerful inner conversation that helps you balance the demands of outer life with inner wisdom (Moore, 1992).

Creative rituals. Simple, powerful rituals can create transformational breakthroughs that nourish your soul. Doing these symbolic acts actively cares for your soul by making space for beauty, music, and art (Moore, 1992).

Integration. Bring together ideas from your inner beloved and integrate them into your conscious life. Regularly consult with your inner parts to foster an attitude of partnership, just like any relationship (Schwartz, 1995).

Listen to symptoms and whispers. The inner self communicates quietly in the low frequencies of dream, imagination, and creative whispers. Listen carefully as your soul speaks to you through moods, dreams, music, longings, or conflicts. Rather than rejecting those things, see them as a message to be honored within your inner dialogue. Greet the messenger gratefully, in whatever form it takes, pay close attention to the message being delivered (Moore, 1992).

Imagination is the bridge. Your imagination, whether through dreams, dialogue, journaling, or creativity, keeps your relationship with your inner beloved alive. If you carry nothing else inside your "cup" in life, this relationship will sustain you and infuse all your outer relationships with soulfulness and meaning (Moore, 1992; Holmes, 2022).

Caring for your soul is an ongoing and never-ending process that honors complexity, ritual, and imagination. Your soul yearns for connection with others. A genuine relationship is a soulful partnership, not just interpersonal contact. Attending compassionately to your symptoms, moods, and even your own suffering, are ways to receive the message from your inner beloved. This relationship will transform you into the authentic person you are already becoming (Moore, 1992).

Creating (Curating) Yourself

It is an act of self-love and care of the soul to tend to the garden of your mind. What you expose yourself to, day in and day out, has a powerful effect on your thoughts, beliefs, and perception of reality. The idea of "you are what you eat" extends more broadly to the concept of "you are what you think."

If something upsets you, stop exposing yourself to it. Put yourself on a "mind diet" and take into yourself the ideas that you want to have. If watching horror movies traumatizes you and leads to panic attacks, stop watching them. If spending too much time on social media is turning you into an internet troll, limit your time in that space.

For example, I got upset with the news recently. Someone suggested that I should find less biased news outlets and be more accepting of news that is not trying to influence my opinion. After a few weeks of neutral news, I had a series of dreams where I was seeing the world differently, like one big planet rather than my little corner of it.

Some of the best ways to improve your mind-diet are to concentrate on things that are healing. Rather than exercising for the perfect body, try walking in nature with your inner beloved and taking beautiful pictures instead. Carefully choose what you put into your mind so that you find your thoughts healing and creative. Cultivate stillness by trying mindfulness practices that quiet the noisy din of the outside world. Relearn to daydream, whether it is sitting in silence, watching the wind blow through the trees, or looking up into the sky and finding shapes in the clouds. Spend time with people or ideas that inspire you.

Meaningful inner dialogue can nourish your world as much as beautiful scenery. Practice gratitude and wonder in your journal. Make a note of remarkable things that catch your attention: clever phrases, interesting art, surprising colors, or tiny acts of kindness. Go back and read your journal again later to learn who you were then and see how much progress you have made (Jung, 1953, 1971; Moore, 1992).

Unplug yourself by making space for slow thinking or spontaneous creativity (Kahneman, 2011). Set boundaries with technology as a kindness towards your soul's well-being. Share something creative, whether it is a suggestion, a gesture of kindness, or a small but thoughtful gift. Acts of kindness feed the soul of the giver and the receiver.

Remember that the sunshine follows the storm. You cannot have the light without the dark. Take care of yourself and have compassion for that lost little girl or boy inside of you who yearns to laugh and play in the sunshine after the rain has stopped.

Forgiving Yourself and Others

"Forgive yourself for not being at peace. The moment you completely accept your non-peace, your non-peace is changed into peace. Anything you accept fully will get you there, will take you into peace. This is the miracle of surrender." – Anonymous, but often attributed to Eckhart Tolle."

Forgive yourself for being human.
Forgive yourself for being imperfect.
Forgive yourself for your suffering.
Forgive yourself and be at peace.

Your inner beloved probably already forgives you for your faults, but it is difficult, sometimes, to accept forgiveness for yourself and others. The most important thing about forgiveness is that it mostly takes place in your own mind, not in-person. Nor are you obligated to fully forgive others who have done terrible things to you, but it is helpful to stop punishing yourself and others so that you can move forward. Otherwise, you end up bitter and unrepentant.

Clients are sometimes extremely angry with those who cared for them as children. I must gently remind clients that people who raise children have a difficult, almost impossible task. Caretakers always make mistakes because they are imperfect, just like the rest of us. When the resentful child grows up, holding onto grudges and long-forgotten mistakes can sour the soul and make the heart bitter. It is important to recognize the difference between mistakes and abuse. Often, it is appropriate for adult children to have compassionate understanding towards their former caretakers. Other times, trauma therapy is required. Either way, forgiveness of self and others is a path towards healing.

Dr. Clarissa Pinkola Estés, the author of *Women Who Run With The Wolves,* prescribes a simple four-step approach for forgiveness (1992):

1. Leave it alone
2. Stop punishing
3. Forget about it
4. Abandon it forever

The last stage is only necessary for you, not for those who committed the offense. If you can let it go, you will be free. Remember that you cannot save someone else's soul, you can only save your own. That is exactly what you should do.

A Lesson: Forgiving

Whether you are forgiving yourself or someone else, here is a script for forgiveness. https://youtu.be/lAhuhoes9M4

1. Begin by sitting comfortably. Close your eyes, breathe deeply and with each exhale, release the tension.

2. When you are fully relaxed, enter your safe space, like a sun-dappled forest clearing, a favorite nook, or a serene sanctuary. Allow your body and mind to relax completely into this haven in your mind.

If at any point you feel overwhelmed or distracted, gently return to your breath and safe place before continuing. Forgiveness is not to be rushed and unfolds naturally in your own time.

3. Say something like this: "I welcome myself into this restful place. All parts of me are welcome here. Whoever needs to speak is safe here in this circle of kindness and acceptance."

Allow all feelings to be present without judgment or urgency. Sometimes, simply creating this safe space is healing itself and may be enough for a session.

4. Give yourself permission to focus gently onto the person, aspect, organization, or entity including yourself with whom you are struggling to forgive. Notice what feelings or images arise.

This step invites curiosity and openness, not forcing forgiveness. If the feelings are too strong or unclear, it is okay to pause here and return when you feel ready.

5. Figures or inner parts may take form. Allow them to speak freely. Imagine the "part that is hurt" and the "part that seeks to forgive" as separate voices. You are the voice that forgives. Or you may simply dialogue with an image or symbol of the thing that needs to be forgiven. You can use your own words, or you can follow the script in this lesson.

Step 1: "Leave it alone."

Forgiver part: *I see how you ache. I see how long you have carried this pain. For now, I invite you to set down your pain, just for a moment. You do not need to fix it. Leave it, gently,* as it is, with no analysis, no justification, no fighting. Rest from it for now. Feel how it feels not to carry the burden.

Wounded Part: *Does leaving it alone mean it will be forgotten?*

Forgiver: *Not at first. Only for this moment we rest. You are not abandoning yourself. You are giving yourself a pause from carrying the weight of this burden.*

If this is the first time you have left this forgiveness alone, stop here. Forgiveness takes time and cannot be rushed. Perform a meaningful ritual that helps you leave the pain alone for a while.

Once you have learned, through forgiveness, to leave it alone, move on to step 2.

Step 2: "Stop punishing."

Forgiver: *Thank you for trying to protect us. It is safe now to stop. I release you from your vigilant watching, from replaying old harm, from believing punishment will restore the balance. Healing happens in gentleness. Punishment cannot change the past. You want to live in the present.*

Wounded Part: *If I stop, will justice be lost?*

Forgiver: *No. The truth stands as it is. We acknowledge the wound, but choose to stop hurting ourselves or others in its name.*

If this is the first time you have stopped punishing yourself or others for this forgiveness topic, stop here. The process of forgiveness requires time and patience. Perform a meaningful ritual that helps you stop punishing yourself or others.

Once you have learned, through forgiveness, to stop punishing yourself and others, move on to step 3.

Step 3: "Forget about it."

Forgiver: *I invite us, with compassion, to turn our gaze from this old wound. We do not need it to define us. We do not deny the pain or what happened, but we choose not to return to it* *again and again. Each memory takes energy that is better spent on new joys. May forgetfulness soften the edges, allowing space for something new.*

Wounded Part: *But what if remembering is all I have left?*

Forgiver: *You are more than the sum of all your pain. Imagine your life where other parts of you can arise, creativity, peace, purpose. You deserve to feel whole again. You deserve to live in the present. You deserve not to be trapped in the past with this pain. Leave it behind you.*

If this is the first time you have allowed yourself to forget this forgiveness topic, stop here. The process of forgiveness requires time and patience. Perform a meaningful ritual that helps you forget about it. This might involve hiding or losing something.

Once you have learned, through forgiveness, to forget about it, move on to step 4 if you feel ready. Forgiving someone forever is not required. Forgiving yourself, however, is the only way you can move past the issue and grow as a person.

Step 4: "Abandon it forever."

Abandoning the issue forever is necessary for yourself but not for others. The issue will probably come back until your inner beloved and you agree to put it to rest forever. Forever is a long time, and you must be patient with yourself.

Forgiver: *Beloved part, we have stayed too long with all this pain. Now, with gratitude for all the lessons pain taught, it is time to release it fully. We place it in a river, or on the wind, or bury it in the earth. It is gone, returned to the great current of life. You are free of it. This story of wrongs and pain no longer binds you to it. Walk forward, unburdened.*

Wounded Part: *Thank you. I can let it go.*

In your mind's eye, see the thing going away forever. Perform a ritual similar to what the forgiver mentioned earlier.

Put something symbolic into the water, or watch it blow away in the wind, or bury it in the ground. Lose it forever.

End the current session, whatever step you are on.

End whatever step you are on. The process of forgiveness takes a long time, so you will need to do this script repeatedly, stopping at different points. It could take a long time.

6. When you are ready, sense the surrounding air in your safe place. Let yourself linger in the peace and forgiveness that you have created. Take several deep breaths, feeling yourself return to your body and mind. Feel the room around you and bring gentle movement to your fingers and toes. When you are ready, open your eyes.

Carry the warmth and clarity of forgiveness back into your daily life, with your full heart, mind, and soul.

Worrying Less and Living More

The biggest problem that most people have is that they worry too much about things that cannot be changed. Worrying less and living more begins with an inner conversation.

Kegan's (1982) insight into spiritual growth encourages you to expand the boundaries of your inner world. You should hold soulful complexity with courage and curiosity (Moore, 1992). In this light, anxiety becomes a message from the soul about your unlived life or neglected values rather than mere mental noise (Hollis, 2005). Your inner beloved supports this evolution, urging patience as you release worries that no longer serve you, because this creates room for presence and meaning. Through this inner dialogue, you can come to understand that self-worth and peace do not depend on controlling things that you cannot change. Instead, you can embrace the fullness of your unfolding inner path with self-compassion.

This loving inner exchange transforms worry into a trusted companion instead of a demanding jailor. With each acknowledgment from your inner beloved, you reclaim your capacity to live freely and move through life's challenges not burdened, but buoyed, by love, awareness, and the knowledge that you are always supported from within. Thus, healing and wholeness are woven into the fabric of your everyday life (Hollis, 2005; Kegan, 1982).

A Lesson: Worrying Less and Living More

Only worry about things that you can control. Worrying about problems that are outside your influence is a fruitless waste of your time and a drain on your personal resources.

Here is a script for worrying less.
https://youtu.be/RhWW2VHCLUc

1. Get comfortable and let your eyes soften and close. Notice your breath as it moves in and out. As you exhale, allow each part of your body to relax a little more until you are ready to proceed.

2. Bring your mind to the one worry that has been circling in your thoughts lately.

This concern is not the entire heap, but just one pebble on your pile of worries.

3. Feel where this worry lives in your body right now: perhaps it is a tension or discomfort in your chest, your throat, or your stomach.

Notice the sensation surrounding this problem without doing anything about it.

4. In your imagination, picture your inner beloved beside you. This presence is wise, steady, and dedicated to helping you. See or sense how they look at you with understanding and compassion, not judgment.

Hear your inner beloved say, gently:

Not every burden is yours to carry. Someone else's hill is not yours to climb. The only soul you can save is your own.

5. In your imagination, invite your inner beloved to reach inside of you and remove this worrying thing that is disturbing you. It is someone else's responsibility, obligation, or fear.

Your inner beloved says:

Thank you. I will take that burden from you, now. You tried, but this is not yours. You can rest easy now.

6. Your inner beloved pulls the worry from inside of you and throws it into the air, where a great bird grabs it and flies away, disappearing into the deep.

7. Your inner beloved says

There is one more thing we need to do. Let us replace what was removed with some things that are better than pointless worries.

8. Your inner beloved hands you a small vial of gratitude and gestures to you. Drink from the small cup and receive the gift of gratitude that your inner beloved has offered to you. Notice how you feel brighter and lighter, like a weight has been lifted from you.

9. Your inner beloved hands you a small vial of compassion. Drink from it and notice how you feel less burdened.

10. Your inner beloved offers you several vials of healing draughts containing tolerance, patience, self-acceptance, courage and other things you so desperately require. You brighten up each time you drink. But not too much: there is no way to make yourself perfect. Make a promise to yourself not to drink anything that belongs to someone else.

Say a quiet word of thanks to your inner beloved for these soulful gifts.

11. In your mind's eye, hold your hands to your heart. Feel these qualities you drank flowing inward and outward, nourishing your spirit and everything around you in your sacred space.

12. Your inner beloved shows you that your inner world is larger now than it was before. It is big enough now to handle the cares that belong to you.

Some things you can influence; and some you cannot. Notice how your body feels as you quietly say

I release what I cannot control. I stay present to what is within my grasp. I make the wise choices that guide my heart and my mind.

13. Make a promise to yourself that if this worry returns to you, you can place it in your inner beloved's hands. This worry is no longer your keeper, it is merely an unwelcome visitor that comes and goes quickly, flying away with that bird like a worm in its beak.

14. Inhale and feel wisdom envelop you. Exhale the tension and the worry that no longer affect you. When you are ready, feel your body where you are and open your eyes. Understand that you can return to this inner conversation any time you want to replace other worries that drain you with soulful healing.

After this inner exercise, I recommend doing an actual ritual with a real cup, to make more permanent replacing these worries with the qualities in those spiritual vials: gratitude, courage, self-awareness, patience, self-acceptance, compassion, and any others, but only if they belong to you.

Healing Family Relationships

Probably the largest source of unconscious shadows comes from your family, where few speak of the dark secrets and untold tales. The relationship that your inner beloved has to your ego's family is the foundation of who you are. Your inner beloved was formed and shaped inside your mind as a reaction to your parents, siblings and significant close relationships that made you who you are today.

The inner beloved is a bridge beyond the family shadow that holds compassion, curiosity, and even leadership over your inner parts that were shaped by your family. You and your inner beloved result from the shadows that your family casts onto you as behavior, projections, and emotional burdens. Your inner beloved can witness these shadows, without judgement, and allow these hidden parts of yourself to be revealed, accepted, and transformed rather than acting them out unconsciously as symptoms of your personal suffering.

Your inner beloved developed not only because of family shadows, but in response to them. Your soul is the guardian and refuge that holds what was rejected and hurt by your family environment. The inner beloved offers you a sacred, safe, wise, and compassionate space where you can find and integrate your family shadow into your authentic self-awareness. Many of those rejected aspects of yourself are actually useful once you have agency as a responsible adult.

There is wisdom within you, representing the deeper layers of your mind, that calls for wholeness. Your inner beloved is the bearer of transformation. Somewhere in there is the pure love and untainted core of who you are that longs for an end to the suffering. You need to meet the family shadow not with fear and resistance or rebellion, but with acceptance, compassion, and creativity. You heal yourself by creating your new self, one strand of gold at a time, repairing the broken pieces of your soul to make something beautiful but imperfect.

The dialogues you have with your inner beloved reflect the light and shadow of "inner work" that your soul needs in order to unite with your higher consciousness (Johnson, 1986). The various parts that are revealed during your transformation are the wounded aspects of your soul that family dynamics created. Broken pieces of you turned into defensive protectors. The dialogues you have with your inner beloved reshape the family narrative that defines who you are becoming, as you transform. You observe where these family wounds have been internalized and consciously decide how to relate differently to these inner voices. Inner defenders become angel saviors and rageful negative parts become warriors in the cause of your "becoming."

Your inner dialogues mend the broken pottery of your psyche into something bonded with gold and clay procured from the bottom of your soul. What results from your dialogues is not perfect, but it is beautiful nonetheless, even with all your flaws and uncertainties (Jung, 1958; Neumann, 1954).

Handling Community Relationships

Your inner self does not relate directly with the local community outside your family, whether it is physical or virtual. Instead, the inner beloved and its parts work with the ego to find appropriate masks of your persona to play social roles and make connections that are crucial in practical, everyday life (Jung, 1953/1966; Neumann, 1954).

Communities have natural expectations for friendships, workplaces, and groups. Your *persona* is the social mask that helps you relate to others in these different contexts with grace and skill. Masks can be useful tools for everyday life. Your inner beloved is still within you, guiding you through self-dialogue to help you balance these outer expectations with curiosity and sensitivity.

When you find yourself reacting negatively to a role or some part of your community, it is time to pause and talk with your inner beloved. Instead of throwing away the mask, try to explore what feels fearful, angry, or false, and integrate that into a stronger, more grounded version of yourself. As people age, they begin to realize that some of these masks are unnecessary. People appreciate and recognize the "real" you far more than the fake masks you obviously wear. Even if you are an amazing actor, being yourself, with certain caveats, is usually better than pretending to be something you are not. Ask yourself, too, whether you belong in a group where wearing a mask is necessary? Changing friends or careers is usually easier than faking your way through an environment that doesn't suit you.

Wearing masks also becomes harmful when people forget they are wearing them. This is the ruin of many successful community leaders, who are typically caught in scandals. They over-identify with their public role and forget about their healthy feelings, relationships, and boundaries. The more authentic self gets pushed into the shadow, where it will fester and return in a fight to re-establish the real self.

Your challenge is to stay self-aware when putting on and taking off masks. Being real with yourself and your intimate companions allows you to continue the honest dialogue with your inner beloved. With each masked performance, you and your inner beloved are acting together and staying aware of who you really are. This allows you to engage creatively with each community that you "dance" with, offering your soulful gifts while respecting the boundaries and rhythms of who you really are (Jung, 1953/1966); Neumann, 1954).

There is wisdom for creative souls in a community. You learn to honor the vulnerable parts of yourself that might resist social masks, such as being shy or anxious. Practising and using humor and pretending like an actor with confidence helps invite your inner self to become a soulful presence in social interactions. This presence creates genuine community participation without losing yourself (Johnson, 1991). My way of contributing to the community and my mental health is to lead Jungian social media groups, do charity work in my community, and vote for community leaders who share my values.

Understanding That the End Is a New Beginning

Probably the most difficult thing about a relationship that ends is trying to admit it's over and that nothing can save it. Whether through neglect, friction, or death, however, every relationship ends. When love cannot be returned, it is a hard lesson to accept (Hollis, 1998, 2005).

I discovered the pain of relationship loss when my father passed away a few years ago. I was having a hard time accepting his death, and I missed our conversations terribly. It was then, in my moment of suffering, that my inner beloved came to me and suggested an inner dialogue to replace the outer conversations I was missing. Talking with my deceased father seemed strange until I remembered visiting a cemetery and seeing visitors standing in front of gravestones, talking, crying, and interacting with their deceased loved ones.

It's important to stay self-aware and open to the next phase of a relationship as it unfolds. But when a relationship cannot continue to grow and thrive, it is over. A relationship cannot die if you are still having a living conversation. But, since they are gone from your outer life, the conversation moves inwards and onwards.

A Letter to Arline from Rich

Richard Feynman, a physics hero of mine who won the Nobel Prize in 1965, lost his wife to tuberculosis in 1945. Richard and Arline were high school sweethearts and married in 1942 despite her illness. He had hoped it was manageable while he worked on the Manhattan Project. He visited her whenever he could sneak away from the facility. She died in June in an Albuquerque sanatorium; he rushed to her side but arrived too late. A movie called *Infinity* starring Matthew Broderick tells the story of the bond of love that they shared in the short time they had together on this Earth.

A year later, Richard wrote a letter, where he struggled to reconcile his scientific realism with his feeling of profound loss for his one true love. After Richard's death in 1988, his family found this letter in his house, unmailed. This letter is an inspirational example of how to maintain a relationship when you have lost someone that you deeply care for.

https://news.lettersofnote.com/p/i-love-my-wife-my-wife-is-dead?utm_source=publication-search

References

Bly, R. (1990). *Iron John: A book about men.* Addison-Wesley.

Burns, R. (1786). To a Louse, On Seeing One on a Lady's Bonnet at Church. In *The poetical works of Robert Burns* (p. 45). Oxford University Press.

Estés, C. P. (1992). *Women who run with the wolves: Myths and stories of the wild woman archetype.* Ballantine Books.

Hillman, J. (1975). *Re-visioning psychology.* Harper & Row.

Hollis, J. (1993). *The middle passage: From misery to meaning in midlife.* Inner City Books.

Hollis, J. (1998). *The Eden project: In search of the magical other.* Inner City Books.

Hollis, J. (2005). *Finding meaning in the second half of life: How to finally, really grow up.* Gotham Books.

Holmes, T. (2022). *Parts work: A path of the heart: Healing journeys integrating IFS and spirituality.* Winged Heart Press.

Johnson, R. A. (1986). *Inner work: Using dreams and active imagination for personal growth.* HarperOne.

Johnson, R. A. (1991). *Owning your own shadow: Understanding the dark side of the psyche.* HarperOne.

Jung, C. G. (1953). *Two essays on analytical psychology* (R. F. C. Hull, Trans., Vol. 7, Collected Works). Princeton University Press.

Jung, C. G. (1958). *Psychology and religion: West and East* (Collected Works of C.G. Jung, Vol. 11, R. F. C. Hull, Trans.). Princeton University Press. (Original work published 1952)

Jung, C. G. (1971). *Memories, dreams, reflections* (A. Jaffé, Ed. & R. Winston, Trans.). Vintage Books.

Kahneman, D. (2011). *Thinking, fast and slow.* Farrar, Straus and Giroux.

Kegan, R. (1982). *The evolving self: Problem and process in human development*. Harvard University Press.

Kimmel, M. S. (2012). *Manhood in America: A cultural history* (3rd ed.). Oxford University Press.

Moore, T. (1992). *Care of the soul: A guide for cultivating depth and sacredness in everyday life*. HarperCollins.

Neumann, E. (1954). *The origins and history of consciousness* (R. F. C. Hull, Trans.). Princeton University Press. (Original work published 1949)

Schwartz, R. C. (1995). *Internal family systems therapy*. Guilford Press.

van den Berk, T. (2012). *Jung on art: The autonomy of the creative drive*. Routledge.
https://doi.org/10.4324/9780203721247

Woodman, M. (1980). *The pregnant virgin: A process of psychological transformation*. Shambhala.

8 Being Creative and Playful

"But if you have nothing at all to create, then perhaps you create yourself." – C. G. Jung (1958)

Your ego receives messages from your inner beloved through creative channels. Take its hand and allow yourself to be safely guided through the chaos of life. Most people have access to creativity in one way or another (Jung, 1968b, 1968d). If you watch little children at play, you are witnessing the birth of their egos (Jung, 1959/1968b). In the early stages, they are almost entirely directed by inner instincts to play with and explore their surroundings.

Artists and creative types are like children at play. They hear the whisper of sacred gifts from the unconscious and make them come to life (Johnson, 1986).

Therapists try to get their clients to "re-engage" with their inner child, which creatively bridges the ego and the inner self. This is a metaphor, of course, because our inner archetypes are certainly not children. But they do exist in the unconscious, in various stages of development, awaiting their next opportunity to send you an important message of guidance (Jung, 1968b).

Appendix C lists the many ways that you can receive guidance from your inner beloved. Restarting that relationship may be easier for some, and more difficult for others. One way to ease back into creative guidance is to make an invitation for playfulness.

A Lesson: Inviting Playfulness

Here is a role-playing conversation that you can have with yourself to invite your inner child to come out and play. https://youtu.be/OXhok0PHdR0

1. Find a quiet space where you can fully relax, using techniques like the ones mentioned in Appendix A.
2. Invite and welcome your inner child parts to come out and play.

Inner playful child, come to me. I need you to remind me of the joys of being young and creative. Come and dance with me, sing with me, laugh and run and play with me. Teach me to play again.

3. Imagine that you are descending the stairs toward your magical play room for creativity. It is a safe place. When you arrive, your playful parts are already there. If you see nothing, entice them to come out and play. Tell them you need a little practice being playful in the real world.
4. Watch in your imagination to see what happens. These meetings with our inner parts depend on your openness and willingness to let yourself be authentic. Remember, there is no one watching except you. Stay and call them until they come even if they are not what you expected. If they are negative or want to control you, do not let them. Ask them to send someone else who is nicer and just wants to play.

If this doesn't work, use your journal to write about your favorite times when you played and enjoyed yourself. Or talk to yourself and listen for your inner playmate to answer. Not necessarily as a voice, but as thoughts that come in response to the inquiry. If you take your ordinary filters off and listen/watch closely, your inner beloved is talking to you.

5. After the session is over, thank the playful parts that came, and tell them they are welcome to come to play with you any time.

One thing that's interesting about all these parts sessions is that unexpected things show up. Sometimes, they speak in words, other times with images, gestures, or feelings (Jung, 1968b). Sometimes ,inner figures will show you unexpected things (Johnson, 1986). Perhaps you all ended up flying instead of playing. Or they might come to you later, in a dream, with vivid and unexpected suggestions (Samuels, Shorter, & Plaut, 1986). Be sure to record those experiences before you forget.

Following the Playful Path to Your Unconscious

We have already discussed dreams, imaginative inner dialogue, and journaling (Johnson, 1986). Other methods of contacting your inner playmate include automatic drawing/writing, creating things with your hands, play therapy, dancing, music, drama, talking to yourself, or just doing whatever creative thing you love to do (Jung, 1964; Kramer, 1977). Listen with all your senses set to maximum for the message, and it will come to you in its own way. Your inner beloved is listening even now, as you read this, trying to tell you something important. Stop for a while each day and listen to what your inner beloved is saying.

The act of creation, whether through music, art, writing, crocheting, or just silly playfulness, opens up a dialogue with your inner world. In analytical psychology, this process is valuable because the unconscious communicates with you while you are in a sort of dreamy state (Jung, 1964). By that, I mean that many creative types find that they "get into the flow" and allow the message to be delivered (Jung, 1968b). Creativity is a loving dance with the unconscious. Often, these messages come to us as stories or fantasies (Johnson, 1986).

For example, writing this book is the way I am currently dancing with my inner beloved. Writing is an act of creation and communion. I just need to be careful not to let the writing and publication process take over my life and ruin all the fun. There is a lot to learn from these inner messages, provided you are careful not to take creativity too seriously.

Creativity asks the ego to surrender and drop all its barriers. Authority and power structures fall away during walking, daydreaming, or spontaneous imagining (Jung, 1964). Ideas come on their own, unbidden, like messages from a timeless place. The less we judge these ideas and simply let them happen, the more healing they can be. Later, we can judge how practical our creativity is in the real world (Christina, 2020; Stein, 1998).

Staying Grounded in Your Soul

The wise counselor realizes that play is not just a childish act, but also, a way to invite the client to learn how to get themselves to the level of their inner beloved (Jung, 1968a). The inner beloved operates at a quieter, lower frequency. People think they need to "go higher" to become enlightened. This is actually dangerous. Ego inflation and possession by the unconscious are common pitfalls of trying to absorb too much unconscious material (Jung, 1954).

The higher you go, the further you get from the soul, which is grounded in you and around you. Your ego emerged from your soul as you matured, with its roots firmly in the unconscious. You get all your ideas from these inner voices. So it is the ego, not the unconscious, that is above. If you try to get too close to the unconscious without being properly grounded in the soul, you will "fall out of the sky" like Icarus, who fell because of his inflated pride.

The soul's grounding symbolizes connection with the unconscious and wholeness. The ego inflates itself by over-exposing itself to unconscious material without proper integration and humility, ignores the warning signs, sails away and eventually crashes to the ground, metaphorically. Jung (1966) says this represents a natural, cyclical process of human psychology that keeps people grounded in reality. A person who crashes from ego inflation typically suffers from nervous breakdowns, failures in their relationships, burnout, social collapse, or an existential crisis.

Understanding Why Art Matters

Why do creative acts matter? Acts of creation engage the unconscious and help you (approach and) transcend the boundaries of your ego. You can expand your awareness, challenge your educated thinking styles, and take the pressure off yourself. These small acts of creation allow your inner voice to emerge safely and authentically. There is no need to pretend to be a genius or a great talent. Just be yourself and try not to let your ego co-opt or talk you out of the talent you have.

Many creative types have found their canvas turned into a prison cell via capitalism. Do your creative work for yourself. If you are fortunate enough to make some money doing it, accept it quietly but do not let financial ideas interfere with your creative process. So many geniuses did one great thing, and then the money-making industry punished them so badly that they never created anything again for fear of the anxiety that success produced. The play instinct is a gift. Do not allow your ego to enslave your creativity with ambitious to-do lists and fantasies of worldly success. The opposite situation is what you want: playfulness should instruct your ego to keep it flexible and self-aware (Marks-Tarlow, 2012). Allow your creativity to be fun and freeing, and it will reward you with a higher quality of life.

Avoiding Traps of Being an Artist

Many talented people fall into the trap of believing, or pretending they are a professional artist. Or, conversely, they perceive that they have no marketable talent, and so they abandon the idea of being creative for practical reasons. Both ideas are incorrect and damaging to inner guidance. A third condition is even worse: being possessed by an inner, negative task-master who will accept nothing less than your perfection under any circumstance.

First, the ego loves to control things and put on masks to impress other people. When I lived in Mendocino County, California, there were a lot of creative people around. But the actual artists were not the ones wearing artist's caps and selling souvenir kitsch to the tourists. Most genuine artists I know wear ordinary clothes and stay in the background, laboring over some meaningful work that their inner beloved has asked them to create.

It is important, while being creative, to ignore any egoistic dreams of fame and fortune. If someone offers you a ton of money to do your art, take it. But do not let your success or lack thereof stop you from moving on to your next creative project. It is important to allow yourself to create things to keep your soul alive. Creativity is liberating and healing.

Second, normal people don't allow themselves to be creative. Most people assume they aren't talented, and so they don't bother being creative (Jung, 1954). But this is a mistake. Almost everyone is creative (Jung, 1964). Or was. The things we are creative at, however, aren't always marketable or appreciated. Still, the inner beloved will send you creative ideas suited to your personality (Johnson, 1986). You must allow yourself to accept these messages regardless of your talent. So many people tell me that they "used to play the piano," or whatever creative thing they did. This makes me sad, because the spark of what makes people interesting and fun is born in their creativity (Stein, 1998). If they quit creating things because it has no practical value, there is a trapped inner artist, banging on the doors of his/her cell, asking to be released.

Finally, the tortured artist is the worst-case scenario for any creative person. Famous artists who lived a life of semi-continuous suffering include Plath, van Gogh, Cobain, and Munch. It is interesting how they all self-harmed. It seems like the greatest artists are possessed by an unwavering, negative taskmaster who will accept nothing less than absolute perfection (Marginalian, 2025). This often happens when they internalize the lessons of an unsympathetic caretaker (Jung, 1964). Something dark and negative possesses most people who suffer mental anguish within their psyche (Perry, 2023).

If you find yourself trapped or tortured by your art, the Observer/Conductor dialogue in Appendix A can help you notice and gently dialogue with that harsh inner part of yourself from a neutral perspective. Inner dialogue is often the first step towards improving your relationship with negative parts.

Doing Ordinary Artsy Things

There are many unprofitable yet important activities that people should do to stay vibrant and in-touch with their inner creative self (Sandford, 2021). This is not an exhaustive list. See Appendix C for further ideas.

Gardening. Many people are amazing gardeners. This was a valuable skill for our ancestors who grew their own food. Having a green thumb is a way to get close to nature. The thoughts we have while gardening are whispers from our inner beloved.

Cooking. Our ancestors were often superb cooks because there weren't any good restaurants around. Cooking is an art. All the thoughts and feelings you have while cooking are messages from your inner beloved.

Sewing, knitting, crocheting. Any form of sewing is a creative act, whether or not it makes money. These small acts of creativity, like making a garment or bedazzling a shirt, are the soul speaking through you and to you.

Being in nature. Mostly what our ancestors did was gather things and be with nature so they could survive in it. Many artists have their greatest ideas in nature while walking, biking, or hiking.

Collecting things. A lot of children collect things, like stamps, coins, dolls, and other collectibles. These things gather dust as we get older, but there is no good excuse for stopping a good collection.

Arranging space. Decorating, Feng Shui, and organizing things is a creative act to make the world around you a more beautiful place. It brings new perspectives into your life. Don't let others stop you from making your world a little more beautiful in your own unique way.

Writing. Even if you aren't great with words or music, the messages need to be taken down so you can receive the wisdom of your inner beloved. No one is expecting you to be a novelist, songwriter, or journalist. Listen and write. Read it later and get a healthy perspective on yourself. Several of my clients have had profound psychological breakthroughs by re-reading their old journal entries.

Drawing. Few people are professional artists, but there is great merit to drawing or coloring while you are at a boring gathering. You can get some pretty interesting ideas while you sit there communing with your inner playmate (Jung, 1964).

Innovating: A Multidisciplinary Approach

"You cannot get educated by this self propagating system in which people study to pass exams, and teach others to pass exams, but nobody knows anything. You learn something by doing it yourself, by asking questions, by thinking, and by experimenting." – Richard Feynman (1999)

The heart and soul of Jungian psychology is the use of creativity to create a new version of your deeper self. This is the process of engaging with your inner beloved to address issues that your ego cannot solve on its own. There is a dance between the unconscious mind that "creates" us, and the ego, which witnesses our creation. As Jung (1968c, para. 391) says, we do not create ourselves, but instead we "happen" to ourselves through our soulful work. People think their ego is in charge, but this is an illusion: your inner self dictates most thoughts and mental activities that manifest themselves in the world. Being aware of this fact helps you live from the inside out, like an artist, rather than from the outside in, like a salesperson.

When Feynman (1999) wrote that "nobody knows anything," he meant that learning for an exam is not learning. Feynman's advice is to take a deep interest in something you love and study it from your soul, like a craftsman. This is the difference between learning at school to pass a test or get a job versus learning to do something for the sheer joy of it. When your curiosity is driven by an inner creative curiosity, you can find soulful healing by learning and creating new things.

Famous innovators who were deeply self-directed learners include Da Vinci, Einstein, Lovelace, Galileo, Franklin, Tesla, and Jobs, to name just a few. Back in the 80s and 90s an academic trend started known as the multidisciplinary approach, which allowed professors to make breakthroughs in their fields by cross-breeding their own ideas with other disciplines. This approach expanded our pattern of innovation to develop breakthroughs, such the Hubble Telescope, RNAi, 3D modeling, artificial intelligence (AI), integrated family therapy (IFT), and cancer research. AI itself uses a multidisciplinary approach that includes linear algebra, neural networks, and other fields (Goodfellow, Bengio & Courville, 2016).

This book itself is actually a result of combining at least four powerful ideas from different specialties: Sufism (the inner beloved concept), Jungian analytical psychology, the Taoist philosophy of finding the inner path, and Internal Family Systems (IFS) parts dialogue. It is by mixing together different specialties that innovators bring us fresh new ideas that have the power to change people's lives.

Using Creativity in Therapy

Jungian practitioners know that any creative act is an opportunity for healing if it is focused on the emotional center of the complex that is troubling their client. The client's unconscious self sends messages via creative acts that are integrated into the ego. Active imagination and IFS parts dialogue are the most common techniques used in creative therapy. But there are other methods that you can do yourself or with the supervision of a therapist (Johnson, 1986).

Art therapy, which involves drawing, painting, journaling, music, dance, mandalas, sand play, and so on, are often used to help convey messages from the client's inner self. Whether or not the client realizes it, their unconscious self is communicating directly to them through any creative act. The inner beloved sends the client messages via creative urges. The only concern is that the ego must not interfere by filtering or censoring the message. Dreams amplification is a common signal, but many cannot remember their dreams. To avoid censoring or filtering the message, clients may need to mute their conscious inner critic for a while using techniques that emphasize curiosity over evaluation (Rubin, 1987).

Mindfulness techniques are often used to enhance self-awareness and allow the client to stay grounded while engaging in unconscious dialogue. This allows the clients to regulate their emotions while deepening their inner connections. Mindfulness can be as simple as remaining present and aware during a dream analysis or active imagination exercise. Clients can learn self-awareness of internal emotional, and external bodily sensations. The ability to become the "objective observer" while interacting with the inner beloved is important, so the client is not overwhelmed or dissociated. This facilitates an authentic dialogue between various parts of the mind. Mindful practices often focus on breathing, paying attention to body sensations, and a witnessing attitude toward thoughts, feelings, and images that emerge during creative sessions with the inner beloved (Kabat-Zinn, 1990).

Somatic therapy addresses body sensations and visible behaviors related to unconscious emotional conflicts, such as tension or sweating. Body work helps integrate mind and body experiences for holistic healing. Thinkers and others who are "too much in their heads," find that body work helps make them feel grounded in their bodies. For many types of clients, the body itself is, literally, unconscious because they do not value or attend to their bodies. Marion Woodman's pioneering work in feminine body work is the gold standard in Jungian somatic therapy (Woodman, 1980). Hillman (1975) wrote about masculine body work. The body remembers what the mind forgets. Somatic healing is a loving dialogue where your soul and body reunite in trust and wholeness.

Jungian healers use narrative, story-based therapy to assist clients with uncovering their inner myths. Everyone has an unconscious, inner story (Jung, 1968b). Knowing the various themes and characters of their inner stories helps clients understand their dreams, and improves the accuracy of interpreting any guidance they receive. Self-talk is one good way to discover their inner stories. Estés' (1992) *Women Who Run With The Wolves* is the gold standard for feminine narrative depth therapy. For men, Johnson's (1991) *He: Understanding Masculine Psychology* and Bly's (1990) *Iron John* uncover the mysteries of the masculine inner narrative. Story-based, narrative approaches to psychotherapy are some of the clearest, most approachable books in psychology. A picture is worth a thousand words, but a story is worth a thousand pictures. Stories mirror your soul's journey, helping to illuminate the hidden patterns and potentials of your inner world.

References

Bly, R. (1990). *Iron John: A book about men.* Addison-Wesley.

Christina M. (2020). Surrender: An alchemical act in personal transformation. *CIIS Journal of Jungian Studies.*

Estés, C. P. (1992). *Women who run with the wolves: Myths and stories of the wild woman archetype.* Ballantine Books.

Feynman, R. P. (1999). *The pleasure of finding things out: The best short works of Richard P. Feynman.* Basic Books.

Goodfellow, I., Bengio, Y., & Courville, A. (2016). *Deep learning.* MIT Press.

Hillman, J. (1975). *Re-visioning psychology.* Harper & Row.

Johnson, R. A. (1986). *Inner work: Using dreams and active imagination for personal growth.* HarperOne.

Johnson, R. A. (1991). *He: Understanding masculine psychology.* HarperOne.

Jung, C. G. (1954). *The development of personality* (R. F. C. Hull, Trans.; Collected works of C. G. Jung, Vol. 17). Princeton University Press. (Original work published 1910–1950)

Jung, C. G. (1958). *Psychology and religion: West and East* (Vol. 11, para. 391 or p. 556). Princeton University Press. (Original work published 1938–1940)

Jung, C. G. (1964). *Man and his symbols.* Doubleday.

Jung, C. G. (1966). *The collected works of C. G. Jung* (Vol. 16, The practice of psychotherapy; 2nd ed.). Princeton University Press. (Original work published 1961)

Jung, C. G. (1966). *The practice of psychotherapy* (Vol. 16, para. 906). Princeton University Press. (Original work published 1946)

Jung, C. G. (1968a). *Psychology and alchemy* (R. F. C. Hull, Trans.; 2nd ed., Collected works of C. G. Jung, Vol. 12). Princeton University Press. (Original work published 1944)

Jung, C. G. (1968b). *The archetypes and the collective unconscious* (R. F. C. Hull, Trans.). In H. Read, M. Fordham, & G. Adler (Eds.), *The collected works of C. G. Jung: Vol. 9, Part 1* (pp. 3-41). Princeton University Press. (Original work published 1959).

Jung, C. G. (1968c). *The collected works of C. G. Jung* (Vol. 11, R. F. C. Hull, Trans.). Princeton University Press. (Original work published 1958)

Jung, C. G. (1968d). *The ego and the unconscious* (R. F. C. Hull, Trans.). In H. Read, M. Fordham, & G. Adler (Eds.), *The collected works of C. G. Jung: Vol. 7* (pp. 1-153). Princeton University Press. (Original work published 1954).

Jung, C. G. (1971). *Psychological Types* (H. G. Baynes, Trans.). Princeton University Press. (Original work published 1921)

Kabat-Zinn, J. (1990). *Full catastrophe living: Using the wisdom of your body and mind to face stress, pain, and illness.* Delta.

Kramer, E. (1977). *Art as therapy with children.* Schocken Books.

Marginalian. (2025). *Carl Jung on creativity.* Retrieved August 30, 2025, from https://www.themarginalian.org/2025/04/09/carl-jung-creativity/

Rubin, J. A. (1987). *Approaches to art therapy: theory and technique.* Brunner/Mazel.

Samuels, A., Shorter, B., & Plaut, F. (1986). *A critical dictionary of Jungian analysis.* Routledge.

Sandford, R. (2021). *A Jungian approach to engaging our creative nature: Imagining the source of our creativity.* Routledge.

Stein, M. (1998). *Jung's map of the soul: An introduction* (3rd ed.). Open Court.

Marks-Tarlow, T. (2012). The play of psychotherapy: Intuition and improvisation in the healing moment. *American Journal of Psychotherapy*, 66(3), 235–250. https://doi.org/10.1176/appi.psychotherapy.2012.66.3.235

Woodman, M. (1980). *The pregnant virgin: A process of psychological transformation*. Shambhala.

9 Practicing Spirituality

John Freeman: "Do you now believe in God?"
Carl Jung: "[Pause] Difficult to answer. I know. I don't need to believe. I know." (1959)

    A powerful, transformative inner experience rescues most people from the problems that assail their souls (Jung, 1968b). Whether you call that profound experience God, the prophet, the inner beloved, or therapy, the name is less important than the healing effect it has upon you (Hillman, 1975). Jung (1968b) acknowledged the ancient wisdom of cultural religions. He stated that having a religious background is usually preferable to having no spirituality at all. Jung (1961, 1968b) found that the deepest healing arises, however, from a personal spirituality rooted in a non-denominational personal spirituality, built upon the foundations of your relationship to your inner psyche.

Saying a Prayer to Your Inner Beloved

    Prayer is a soulful dialogue and a gentle invitation to commune with your inner beloved that awakens symbolic wisdom and insight (Jung, 1954; Johnson, 1986). Prayer in this context is spiritual, not religious. The effectiveness of prayer lies primarily in its ability to change how you think and to conjure creative, symbolic dialogue and insight. People can and should dialogue with themselves soulfully using inner prayer to integrate their shadows.

I sometimes say a prayer before I sleep to send a message and begin a dialogue with my inner beloved. My devotional prayers ask questions and seek guidance and understanding that my conscious ego genuinely needs. That's why I choose my topics carefully. If you say a prayer that is meaningful and important to you, it is likely that your inner beloved will take note and reply with an answer in its ancient language. Whether you can understand the answer is a matter of sitting with the resulting thoughts and images until you obtain a fresh idea. This is similar to how you interpret a dream or an imaginative dialogue.

Here is a variation on the 'prayer to the inner self' from earlier. It is a good lesson on how to say a prayer to your inner self and ask for guidance. At the end, be sure to add your specific inquiry, which is focused on a single concern.

https://youtu.be/pf73r5MXpW4

> *O heavenly Inner Beloved,*
> *Please receive my thanks for your guidance,*
> *Past, present, and future.*
> *Please accept my friendship with open arms.*
> *Please accept my apologies for my imperfections,*
> *That I may always seek balance and self-awareness*
> *In my body and my soul.*
> *I seek enlightenment*
> *I seek guidance.*
> *Let us walk together as one*
> *Forever and ever*
> *Tonight, I ...*
> *Blessed be our sacred relationship,*
> *Amen.*

Distinguishing Spirituality from Religion

Spirituality is the personal expression of our own inner relationship to self. Religion happens in society when that personal expression is taught to others to spread that same inspiration. Shared spirituality in a clan is how ancient humans came together for a common purpose to help one another and ensure the survival of the group. The lessons they passed down from ancient stories contain the wisdom of the human race.

Religion can serve as healing therapy when you are deeply invested to integrate your participation into a meaningful, soulful experience. Jung (1968a) and others suggest that when you genuinely internalize and personalize religion, it can help individuals cope with trauma, anxiety, and depression by fostering a sense of meaning and purpose in life (Smith, McCullough, & Poll, 2003; Koenig, 2012). I witnessed this personally as a youth while serving as an acolyte in St. Anne's Episcopal church in Linden, California. The priest, Father Thompson, let me participate as an acolyte even in services that did not actually need an acolyte. This early experience gave me a strong "felt" sense of the sacred that set me apart from my peers. From this experience, I understood how an outstanding spiritual leader can make all the difference in your inner growth.

The difficulty in modern times is that religion is no longer central to the lives of most people (Cashwell, Bentley & Bigbee, 2010; Masters, 2010). Even when people attend church, the stories and imagery of sacred texts have to be translated, interpreted and made personally meaningful before they can truly touch the soul. Usually, our rational minds turn these living stories into school lessons that are analyzed, compartmentalized, and stripped of their deeper meaning. I often recite a prayer in church, but I sense that my soul and emotions remain untouched.

Jung (1968a) preferred personal spirituality over religion because it connects to your individual soul. Healing happens when you engage in a creative, authentic inner journey with your inner beloved.

It concerns me that archaic admission rules often exclude certain types of people from joining this or that religion. Several friends have confided to me that they no longer feel welcome in their childhood's religion because their lifestyle does not conform to the strict rules of who can be saved according to dogma. Flawed interpretations and local prejudices so often distort the accurate teachings and practices of the prophets. That is why a great religious leader is so valuable in a community.

Since fewer modern people are interested in the religious institutions of today, therapy is a reliable alternative. There is research proving the effectiveness of psychological healing approaches. This text presents a Sufi-based (mystical inner communion with the divine beloved) approach to inner guidance using imaginative IFS parts dialogue. IFS therapy has growing empirical support. Studies reported by Schwartz (2014) show significant reductions in PTSD and depressive symptoms, with most participants no longer meeting PTSD criteria at a one-month follow-up. Those healing effects, including the empirical feedback from my own clients, are the reason I have sought to publish this book.

Making Spirituality Your Religion

"There are two kinds of fools: those who take religion literally, and those who think it has no value." – Anonymous

Your personal spirituality is the sacred conversation that you conduct with your inner beloved. This living relationship is the heart of your unique, flowering personal religion. Religion is someone else's spirituality, written and practiced by them. Personal spirituality is simply the conversation that people have with their inner beloved that begins their soulful journeys to personal transformation. To say it more plainly, people have their foundational beliefs, and those act as their personal religion, regardless of their membership in a formal religion (Johnson, 1986, Jung 1968a).

Spirituality can be the medicine for the modern malaise of the hyper-rational world. The spiritual path is not an escape from the world, but instead a conscious engagement with our soul, or inner beloved (Johnson, 1986, Jung 1968a). Your inner conversation provides balance and gives you the strength and courage to face the physical world.

If you cannot find your way to a particular religion or faith, I encourage you to practice your own personal spirituality in your conversations with your inner beloved. Not only does private spirituality make sense, it becomes unavoidable. People have inner conversations whether or not they realize it.

This inner voice is what Tolle (1999) called the authentic voice of awareness. Neurobiologists such as Damasio (1999) have shown that this sense of self and inner narrative comes from integrated brain-body processes that are beyond our ego's control. Your ego witnesses that voice, but it comes from a deeper place of guidance in the unconscious mind. With self-awareness, this conversation becomes conscious and directs your life like Dorothy following the yellow brick road.

We all have personal rituals, such as a daily walk, lighting a candle when we meditate, keeping a journal, or setting an intention for the day's tasks. We also have creative acts of the soul that we do too, whether in service to others or for personal expression. Through these small acts, each person engages in his/her own sacred rites, constructing a meaningful spiritual life that is most easily described as organized personal spirituality (Jung, 1968a; Stein, 1998).

Having a Profound Experience Will Heal You

You will find healing when you embrace your own depths. Your inner beloved will speak through profound, soul-touching experiences.

When people reach their lowest point, they find something. Or, more accurately, something finds them. When people have finally reached into their own depths, they will hear an autonomous unconscious force, the inner beloved. People who undergo change and healing often report having a profound experience. Jung (1961, 1968b) and others have stated that spiritual transformation and healing does not happen because of a profound faith, but because of a profound experience. After the fact, such experiences draw people toward a culturally approved faith (Jung, 1968b).

When I am working with clients, I am attempting to provoke them into a profound experience that relieves the pain they are experiencing. Healing is the living word engraved upon people's souls, whispered in divine symbolic experiences rather than dry doctrine. A profound experience comes to people and heals them (Jung, 1964, 1969). This might happen to a client in a dream, for instance, in the image of a wounded animal transforming into a wise guide, suddenly revealing buried grief that dissolves a long-held trauma. It is fascinating to me that while the body heals through medicine, the mind heals through symbolism.

In the ancient world, symbolic healing is what shamans and gurus did (Eliade, 1964). Today, we understand the mind better and realize that a profound experience heals people. A powerful experience will heal them more effectively because it is real and personal. Luckily, the human genome supplies people with an inner healer that can provide them with a genuinely healing transformation that provides them with the fresh perspective they need (Jung, 1968a; Roesler, 2023).

Encountering the Self

"The Kingdom of God is Within You." – Leo Tolstoy (1893/2025)

Encountering the Self is a sacred gift, often a divine or numinous presence that inspires awe and invites transformation, sometimes gently, sometimes dramatically. People encounter the Self in dreams and visions as a visit from a prophet or God, a mandala symbol, a wise old man or woman, or some other archetype that is clearly not a part of their personal memories. The Self represents everything that people are body, mind, and soul. Jung (1966) suggests that all humans possess a Self archetype. Neurobiologists and cultural anthropologists agree (Fontanari & de Oliveira, 2017; Campbell, 1949).

A natural encounter with the Self can happen through meditation, guided imagery, mindfulness, dreams, or spontaneous inner experiences. Encounters with the Self are a rare but unmistakable experience. An encounter with the Self profoundly changed people (Jung, 1966; 1968a). A Self encounter can be a jarring wake-up call for transformative change (Jung, 1953, 1968a; Kiehl, 2024). It affects who we are, how we perceive reality, and the deeper parts of our spirituality. An encounter with the Self is like tripping without the drugs.

It is important to note that both Jung and modern therapists do not recommend drug-induced encounters with the Self outside a controlled medical setting. Medical experiments to treat PTSD and chronic depression are promising. Psychedelic experiences in an uncontrolled environment, however, offer no realistic way to come down safely during a bad trip.

Rather than a jolt of lightning, however, an encounter with the Self can also be the slow "drip drip" of multiple gentle experiences that span through your lifetime. It is hard, sometimes, to tell whether it is the whole Self or some part, like your inner beloved, who has come calling to guide you.

I had two encounters with the Self. In both, Jesus came to me in a vision before I turned 15. In the first, a book meant to help children deal with death caused me a great deal of anxiety. The blonde Jesus from the book came to me in an unforgettable encounter and scared me badly, because I thought I had died, and he was coming to take me to heaven. In the second encounter, Christ spoke to me from the woods while I lay sleeping in a camper. He told me that he was always here, in the deep woods, waiting for me. Between those encounters and my own early religious experiences in church, I was never the same.

People who encounter the Self archetype often turn to religion or therapy, and that seems appropriate. An encounter with the Self can be as traumatizing as it is healing (Johnson, 1986; Jung, 1960; Zweig, 1997). Having an encounter with the Self is powerful, and not everyone can withstand the voltage. I was terrified of dying after my first encounter. My relationship with my inner self began after my second encounter, when Jesus came to me in a dream and invited me to talk with him in the forest.

If you are reeling from an encounter with your greater Self, there are priests, coaches, and therapists who can help you find your way forward. The most important thing to do when the Self comes is to answer the call. But you do not have to do it alone.

Facing the Soul Instead of Worshiping False Gods

"People will do anything, no matter how absurd, to avoid facing their own souls." – C. G. Jung (1968b)

False gods, according to Jung (1953), are addictive obsessions that people turn to when they are in crisis and are desperate to end the suffering. Addictions with harmful effects include substances, politics, sex, social media, gambling, shopping, eating, working, and relationships (to name a few).

The soul calls us to awareness. Interacting with our soul helps us avoid the quick fixes and false gods that society offers. True healing grows from heartfelt inner work and soulful presence. These obsessions are only temporary measures that temporarily relieve the pain. Soon enough, however, they lead to depression, anxiety and addiction. Inner spirituality is the "true god" that is best at achieving lasting inner peace and mental balance (Woodman, 1982).

You can achieve sustainable inner growth using mindful practices, inner dialogue, and symbolic ritual. These practices help you integrate the shadow with the ego (Jung, 1966). True healing and resilience come from cultivating practices that engage and nurture the soul rather than evade it. Developing personal spirituality, honest inner dialogue, creative expression, and meaningful service can offer sustainable personal growth. These approaches foster qualities essential to psychological health: self-compassion, clear boundaries, authentic connection, and a rich inner life (Jung, 1968a).

Johnson (1997) explains that wholeness emerges from the creative attention between spirit (heaven) and soul (earth). He illustrates how his own life found balance not through rigid control or escapism, but by honoring his inner beloved alongside the demands of daily life. Johnson teaches that true balance is a sacred marriage of opposites that prevents the soul from becoming lost in abstraction or material obsessions. False gods, he says, are one-sided distortions of heaven and earth, whereas authentic personal growth flows from using patient inner dialog between our highest ideals and grounded reality.

By shifting the focus away from external distractions to internal awareness, you can open up the possibility of genuine transformation that embraces the entire self to a life that is grounded in reality rather than illusion.

Focusing on Your Own Sacred Conversations

Having a dialogue with your inner beloved provides you with companionship, guidance, and spirituality that manifests as inner truth. Your inner dialogues, dreams and awe-filled encounters hold profound personal truths that are tuned uniquely to your soul. They come from within just for you. You should treasure them as the most intimate sources of spiritual guidance.

I encourage my clients to have dialogues with their inner beloved because those experiences are subjectively real and personal to them. Jung (1966) says that subjective experiences are just as real and probably more personally relevant than anything that occurs in the physical world. Just because something literally happens does not make it meaningful. If only outer events mattered, therapy would not work. Inner dialogue can transform people's lives profoundly, especially if it hits you hard, like a transformative insight.

It is important to prioritize your own actual, lived inner experiences over those of someone else's experiences. I'm talking about your own dreams, intuitions, imaginings, synchronicities, and moments of awe as the primary source of your spiritual guidance. You need to reflect on the powerful inner events that have happened to you, not someone else. The events described in some other text are not yours. While sacred texts tell wise stories, your healing will arise authentically from your own inner journey, as intimate and unique as your own heartbeat (Johnson, 1986). If you are a powerfully religious person, these insights will mix with your faith's beliefs uniquely to speak to you as only your inner beloved can.

I cannot count the number of healing tears that have flowed from mine and my clients' own dialogues with their inner beloved. You need to concentrate on your own journey. Do not be distracted by the path that other people take. Yours is a unique journey: be guided from within and follow your path to personal transformation (Fowler, 1981; Shamdasani, 2012). Even if you are guided by a sacred text, your inner beloved will connect you with it at a personal level that transcends any book or sermon. All you need to do is listen and enter into a sacred inner dialogue.

There is a delicate balance between the outer beauty of nature and inner conversation that inspires people and opens up them to transformation. When people are talking about their own way to freedom, their experiences are not yours. The glory of someone else's triumphant transformation is their journey. To worship another's path avoids your own. Whatever opens you up and begins your inner growth is what you should do.

Being in Service to Others

Serving others is a radiant expression of a healed soul that nourishes connections, has purpose, and holds compassion towards others. Service to others is not just a choice, it is a mentally healthy lifestyle (Greenleaf, 1977).

I was forever changed after I spent two years volunteering to answer phones for the Crisis Line for the Champaign County Mental Health organization. By helping others in their moments of desperate need, I became aware of the duty I had to the healing of my own soul. Later in life, I continued to heal myself by volunteering with civic service organizations, such as the Rotary Club, and non-profit community services, like the YMCA.

Science reveals that acts of kindness release healing neurochemicals, which uplift both the giver and receiver in a sacred dance of care. It is not just "doing good deeds" and the feelings of satisfaction in doing them. Service to others creates real psychological and emotional benefits that work with other positive habits. Service to others promotes spirituality, self-awareness, creativity, and inner dialogue (Hui, et al., 2020).

Helping others has been shown to release "feel good" neurochemicals, such as oxytocin, dopamine and endorphins, which lift mood and combat stress and depression. Since service to others does not pay well, you may need to dedicate a percentage of your free time outside of work to doing service for others. Studies have shown that acts of service, no matter how large or small, lower stress hormones and lead to improved emotional equilibrium (Brown, et al., 2013; Fryburg, 2021).

People who do good works for others report a sense of purpose in their lives. Helping others makes people feel needed and valued. A sense of being connected to something larger than yourself will combat feelings of loneliness and loss of meaning. Forster (1910, 1923) wrote *Howard's End* and *A Room with A View,* exploring themes of human connection, empathy, and bridging social divides. *A Passage to India* (1924) widens that idea to embrace cross-cultural understanding. Human connection is essential for humans to flourish. I have found that message important to my own spiritual development.

Building connections almost always involves interaction, which reduces isolation and creates authentic relationships. These kinds of bonds, however temporary, will live on in your memory long after the encounter. Connections are wonderful buffers against personal stress, anxiety and depression. Feelings of belonging to a cause greater than your own gives your life meaning and purpose (Ryff & Singer, 1998).

Serving others helps people feel like they are part of a larger whole. This reinforces feelings of being connected. Being connected is the cornerstone of many spiritual practices. Spiritual traditions highlight how service is a path toward self-transcendence, compassion, and a deeper relationship with the inner beloved or higher self (Impact Vision, 2024).

If you serve others, this provides you with a new perspective on the challenges that other people have. It puts you in contact with people who are in need. Serving those in need will help overcome your personal biases and assumptions because these are real people with actual problems. Meeting and knowing people with genuine needs helps humanize them (Batson, 2011).

I did several years of service through the Rotary Club by delivering food to Native Americans. I have visited these people in their land, heard their stories, and understood how my donation positively affected their lives. This experience profoundly changed my perspective of native peoples around the world.

When you are helping others, you are usually doing it on a shoestring budget. A lack of money gives people the motivation to find creative solutions through flexible thinking and creative problem-solving. If you run out of boxes to deliver food, you end up talking to retailers who have extra boxes that they normally just throw away. The less money you have to solve a problem, the more creative you are forced to be in order to do service for others (Fink, 2012; Stokes, 2005). It is interesting how being poor actually fosters creativity because the poor must "make do" with what little they have.

As you provide service for others, you may wonder why you are drawn to help them. You learn about yourself, your strengths and weaknesses as a volunteer. Self-reflection will often reveal your own unexplored values, hopes, and opportunities for future growth. Knowing yourself better helps you understand how you can be a better human being. You may find a calling while in service to others (Kawai, 2021).

Achieving Self-Awareness

Self-awareness is the gentle light from within that reveals our shadows, opening the way for forgiveness of self and others. Good mental health begins with self-awareness. Self awareness is the cradle of self-care and compassion towards others. Noticing the soft whisper within us begins the process of conversing with and integrating your shadow. This gives you a healthy humility, because none of us is perfect. Since everyone is capable of terrible things, you can start by forgiving yourself for the harmful things you have done. If you can forgive yourself, you can learn to forgive others and move forward with a sense of tolerance (Woodman, 1982). To stay in balance with your inner beloved, you will need to continue learning lessons of humility and personal improvement throughout your lives. But you can also teach others and serve humanity (Wagani & Gaur, 2024).

Self-awareness is the foundation of emotional well-being and resilience. By knowing what you are thinking and feeling consciously, you gain insight into yourself and how to live a more balanced, authentic life (Wagani & Gaur, 2024).

When you notice your own thoughts and feelings, you can guard against being swept away by them. This allows you to improve your responses to stressors. When bad things happen, most people lose focus and get anxious and angry. If you notice your own thoughts, you can control your reactions. Over time, self-awareness builds resilience. Inner strength grows from a compassionate presence with your inner wholeness, allowing grace amid life's challenges. Inner strength to withstand the world makes it easier for you to cope with the inevitable setbacks in life (Van der Meulen, et al., 2022). If you can learn to walk through the fire of chaos while staying focused, you can do anything.

When you can regulate your reaction to stressors, this improves your mood because you know that you can handle problems. You will not need to worry about being worried any more (Wagani & Gaur, 2024).

The ability to notice your thoughts and handle stress will begin to improve the choices you make. You know who you are, and you know your values and needs and goals. Now, because you know you can handle it, you can make better, more deliberate and meaningful choices. You no longer make choices out of fear or worry, but from knowledge and experience drawn from self-awareness (Brown & Smith, 2014). Eventually, you make your own choices, whereas before your choices were making you.

Once you are aware of your strengths and weaknesses, this allows you to recognize your own personal struggles. You can start to see yourself objectively, without judgment or shame. This paves the way for more self-acceptance and forgiveness. You are no longer driven by some impossible taskmaster that requires perfection because you know that no one, least of all yourself, is perfect. Once you do not expect perfection from yourself, you are no longer driven to expect it from others. This leads to compassion for yourself and others, which makes you much easier to deal with (Woodman, 1982).

Compassion is the gateway to self-care. It is difficult to be good to others until you are good to yourself. You cannot be good to yourself until you have compassion and forgiveness for yourself. Once you realize you aren't perfect, it is possible to take care of yourself and those around you. Caring for your soul from within is the beginning of meaningful caring and connection toward others around you (Prakash & Verma, 2024).

Being self-aware allows you access to your inner thoughts, which are the source of human creativity. Creativity is whispered wisdom from our inner beloved's lips. A soulful inner conversation guides you towards becoming who you are from the inside out. By allowing yourself to listen, with self-awareness, to the creative voice of your inner beloved, you become aware of the power of your imagination. Allowing yourself to be creative is the best way to understand yourself and consciously receive messages from your inner beloved that help you move forward to the next great challenge in life. There are always and forever new challenges in life. Do that creative thing that you do which allows you to hear the inner messages being sent to you. This is your inner beloved whispering and guiding you (Henriksen, Richardson & Shack, 2020).

References

Batson, C. D. (2011). *Altruism in humans*. Oxford University Press.

Brown, K., & Smith, L. (2014). The role of self-awareness in effective decision making. *Journal of Applied Psychology*, 99(6), 1123-1135. https://doi.org/10.1037/a0037467

Brown, S. L., Nesse, R. M., Vinokur, A. D., & Smith, D. M. (2013). Giving to others and the association between stress and mortality. *Psychological Science*, 24(9), 1523-1529. https://doi.org/10.1177/0956797613475631

Campbell, J. (1949). *The Hero with a Thousand Faces*. Princeton University Press.

Cashwell, C. S., Bentley, J., & Bigbee, K. A. (2010). Spiritual bypassing: When spirituality disconnects us from what really matters. *Counseling and Values*, 55(2), 140-153. https://doi.org/10.1002/j.2161-007X.2010.tb00073.x

Damasio, A. (1999). *The feeling of what happens: Body and emotion in the making of consciousness*. Harcourt.

Eliade, M. (1964). *Shamanism: Archaic techniques of ecstasy* (W. R. Trask, Trans.). Princeton University Press.

Fink, A., et al. (2012). *Stimulating creativity via the exposure to other people's ideas*. Human Brain Mapping. https://www.ncbi.nlm.nih.gov/pmc/articles/PMC6870350/

Fontanari, J. F., & de Oliveira, S. M. (2017). The affective core of the Self: A neuro-archetypical perspective on Jung's theory. *Frontiers in Psychology, 8*, Article 1424. https://doi.org/10.3389/fpsyg.2017.01424

Forster, E. M. (1910). *Howards End*. Edward Arnold.

Forster, E. M. (1923). *A room with a view*. A.A. Knopf.

Forster, E. M. (1924). *A passage to India*. Grosset & Dunlap.

Fowler, J. W. (1981). *Stages of faith: The psychology of human development and the quest for meaning.* Harper & Row.

Fryburg, D. A. (2021). Kindness as a stress reduction–health promotion intervention: A review of the psychobiology of caring. *International Journal of Environmental Research and Public Health, 18*(4), Article 1533. https://doi.org/10.3390/ijerph18041533

Greenleaf, R. K. (1977). *Servant leadership: A journey into the nature of legitimate power and greatness.* Paulist Press.

Henriksen, D., Richardson, C., & Shack, K. (2020). *Mindfulness and creativity: Implications for thinking and learning.* Educational Philosophy and Theory, 52(10), 971-982. https://doi.org/10.1080/00131857.2020.1737458 (also available at https://pmc.ncbi.nlm.nih.gov/articles/PMC7395604/)

Hillman, J. (1975). *Re-visioning psychology.* Harper & Row.

Hui, B. P. H., & colleagues. (2020). Prosocial behavior and well-being: A meta-analytic review. *Psychological Bulletin.* https://doi.org/10.1037/bul0000225

Impact Vision. (2024). *Growing spiritually through Christian service.* https://impact.vision/blog/growing-spiritually-through-christian-service/

Johnson, R. A. (1986). *Inner work: Using dreams and active imagination for personal growth.* Harper & Row.

Johnson, R. A. (1997). *Balancing heaven and earth: The art of daily life.* HarperSanFrancisco.

Jung, C. G. (1953). *Two essays on analytical psychology* (R. F. C. Hull, Trans., Vol. 7, Collected Works). Princeton University Press.

Jung, C. G. (1959, October 22). *Face to Face* [Television interview]. BBC Television. Interviewed by John Freeman.

Jung, C. G. (1961). *Memories, dreams, reflections* (R. F. C. Hull, Trans.). Vintage Books. (Original work published 1962)

Jung, C. G. (1964). *Man and his symbols.* Doubleday.

Jung, C. G. (1966). *The structure and dynamics of the psyche* (Collected Works of C. G. Jung, Vol. 8, R. F. C. Hull, Trans.). Princeton University Press. (Original work published 1960)

Jung, C. G. (1968a). *A study in the process of individuation* (R. F. C. Hull, Trans.). In H. Read, M. Fordham, & G. Adler (Eds.), *The collected works of C. G. Jung: Vol. 9* (Part 1) (pp. 1-289). Princeton University Press. (Original work published 1916-1954)

Jung, C. G. (1968b). *Psychology and alchemy* (Vol. 12, para. 126). Princeton University Press.

Jung, C. G. (1977). *C. G. Jung speaking: Interviews and encounters* (E. O'Neill, Ed.). Princeton University Press. (Original work published year varies)

Kiehl, E. (2024). The transcendent function. *International Association of Analytical Psychology.* https://iaap.org/jung-analytical-psychology/short-articles-on-analytical-psychology/the-transcendent-function/

Jung, C. G. (1968). *The ego and the unconscious* (R. F. C. Hull, Trans.). In H. Read, M. Fordham, & G. Adler (Eds.), *The collected works of C. G. Jung: Vol. 7* (pp. 1-153). Princeton University Press. (Original work published 1954)

Jung, C. G. (1969). *Confrontation with the Unconscious. In The structure and dynamics of the psyche* (Collected Works of C. G. Jung, Vol. 8, R. F. C. Hull, Trans., pp. 170-199). Princeton University Press. (Original work published 1960)

Jung, C. G. (2009). *The Red Book: Liber Novus* (S. Shamdasani, Ed. & Trans.). W. W. Norton & Company.

Johnson, R. A. (1986). *Inner work: Using dreams and active imagination for personal growth*. Harper & Row.

Johnson, R. A. (1993). *Owning your own shadow: Understanding the dark side of the psyche*. HarperOne.

Kawai, T. (2021). A theoretical framework on reflection in service learning: Deepening reflection through identity development. *Frontiers in Education*, 6, Article 604997. https://doi.org/10.3389/feduc.2020.604997

Masters, R. A. (2010). *Spiritual Bypassing: When Spirituality Disconnects Us From What Really Matters*. Conari Press.

Moore, T. (1992). *Care of the Soul: A Guide for Cultivating Depth and Sacredness in Everyday Life*. HarperCollins.

National Center for PTSD. (2017, October 2). Mindfulness-based treatments for posttraumatic stress disorder (PTSD). *U.S. Department of Veterans Affairs*. https://www.ptsd.va.gov/professional/treat/txessentials/mindfulness_based.asp

Prakash, S., & Verma, S. K. (2024). Psychological interventions to promote self-forgiveness: A systematic review. *BMC Psychology*, 12, Article 157. https://doi.org/10.1186/s40359-024-01671-3

Roesler, C. (2023). The process of transformation—the core of analytical psychology. *Journal of Analytical Psychology*, 68(2), 217-237. https://doi.org/10.1111/1468-5922.12815

Ryff, C. D., & Singer, B. (1998). The contours of positive human health. *Psychological Inquiry*, 9(1), 1-28. https://doi.org/10.1207/s15327965pli0901_1

School of Mary. (2025). *Jungian personality types and qualities conducive to spiritual direction*. Retrieved July 8, 2025, from https://schoolofmary.org/jungian-personality-types-and-qualities-conducive-to-spiritual-direction/

Schwartz, R. C. (2014). Internal Family Systems therapy: New dimensions. *International Journal of Internal Family Systems Therapy*, 1(1), 15-28.

Shamdasani, S. (Ed.). (2012). *The Cambridge companion to Jung*. Cambridge University Press.

Shamdasani, S. (2014). *Commentary on Jung's Red Book*. The Santa Barbara Independent.

Stokes, P. D. (2005). *Creativity from constraints: The psychology of breakthrough*. Springer Publishing.

Tolle, E. (1999). *The power of now: A guide to spiritual enlightenment*. New World Library.

Tolstoy, L. (1894). *The kingdom of God is within you* (C. Garnett, Trans.). The Cassell Publishing Company.

Van der Meulen, M. M. M., et al. (2022). Parallel changes in positive youth development and self-awareness: Emotional self-regulation and self-esteem positively associated with resilience and psychological wellbeing. *Prevention Science*, 23(2), 242-253. https://doi.org/10.1007/s11121-022-01345-9

Wagani, R., & Gaur, P. (2024). Role of self-awareness in the promotion of health and well-being of college students. *Archives of Depression and Anxiety*, 10(1), 001-011. https://doi.org/10.17352/2455-5460.000086

Woodman, M. (1982). Addiction to perfection: The still unravished bride: A psychological study. Inner City Books.

Zweig, C., & Wolf, S. (1999). *Romancing the shadow: Illuminating the dark side of the soul*. Ballantine Books.

Using Mindfulness Techniques

After you get into a conversation with the inner beloved (Johnson, 1986), there are three participants: the active ego, the objective observer, and the inner beloved. Eckhart Tolle (1999; Kabat-Zinn, 1994) explains how we are more than just our ego thoughts. We are actually the observer of those thoughts. Jung (1966) pointed out the value of a relationship between ourselves and our inner beloved.

This way of being and understanding is not just theory, this is how it works in real life. People try to identify as the calm watcher to avoid the stressful traps of the outer ego and the impossible perfectionism of the inner self.

A Lesson: Simple Box Breathing

Box breathing is a simple, powerful technique for calming the mind and centering yourself. You can do this before each script in the text by making an invitation to your inner beloved. This practice can help you create a gentle, receptive space for self-connection and loving-kindness (Kabat-Zinn, 1994). https://youtu.be/ZQvnlxTRzyM

1. Find your space. Sit or lie down comfortably. Place one hand on your chest and another on your belly to feel your breathing.

2. Silently set your intention. Perhaps you want to invite your inner beloved to be with you at this moment. "I am open to meeting my inner beloved."

3. Visualize the box. Imagine a gentle, glowing square in your mind's eye. Each side of the box represents a phase of your breath.

4. Begin the breath cycle.

    a. Inhale slowly through your nose to a count of four, tracing up one side of the box, like drawing in warm, loving energy.

    b. Hold your breath for four counts, moving across the top of the box. Feel the loving energy settling in your heart.

    c. Exhale gently through your mouth for four counts, tracing down the other side of the box. Imagine releasing any tension or self-judgment.

5. Continue this cycle (in four, hold four, out four) from the top of your head to the bottom of your toes, until each part of your body is very relaxed.

6. Optional: During each phase, you could silently repeat a gentle phrase to yourself to deepen your invitation to your inner beloved:

    a. Inhale: *I welcome my inner beloved.*

    b. Hold: *I rest in your loving presence.*

    c. Exhale: *I release what no longer serves me.*

    d. Hold: *I am open to love within.*

7. Have an inner conversation. Or just be there, experiencing relaxation.

8. Close the exercise. When you feel ready, let your breath return to normal. Sit quietly for a little while, noticing any sensations or feelings that arise. If you had an inner conversation, thank them for the talk and write something in your journal.

This box breathing exercise not only calms and centers you but also creates a mindful, loving space that is perfect for starting your conversation with your inner beloved.

A Lesson: Simple Meditation

Meditation is a simple, powerful way to connect with your inner self and bring a little more calm and clarity into your life. Here is a simple lesson in meditation that anyone can try. There is no special equipment or experience required. The goal is to pause, breathe, and become more aware of your mind and body (APA, 2019; Mayo Clinic, 2023).
https://youtu.be/-MybrXtKPjw

1. Find a quiet, comfortable spot to sit. Be upright but relaxed, with your hands resting in your lap or on your knees.
2. Set a timer. Start small for just two to five minutes. As you gain confidence, you can increase the time.
3. Close your eyes gently or keep them softly focused on a spot in front of you.
4. Take a few deep breaths, in through your nose and out through your mouth. Let your breath settle into a natural, relaxed rhythm.
5. Do a quick body scan from head to toe, observing any tension or discomfort. If you need more time to relax, go ahead.
6. Bring your attention to your breath. Feel the sensation of breathing in and out. Perhaps count your breaths up to ten, then start over at one.
7. When your mind wanders (and it will), notice the thought and gently bring your attention back to your breath. There is no need to judge.
8. After your timer goes off, take a moment to notice how you feel before moving on with your day. Increase the time later as you gain more experience with meditation.

Beginners do not need to worry about "doing it right." Just showing up for yourself is enough. Try to meditate at the same time each day to make it a habit. If you want to explore further, there are many books, apps and online resources available for further study and practice. I recommend the works of Jon Kabat-Zinn (1994), Headspace (2023), or Tara Brach (2012) for more comprehensive guidance.

A Lesson: Basic Active Imagination

This text uses active imagination techniques combined creatively with Internal Family Systems (IFS) parts dialogue to connect and converse with your inner beloved. This inner dialogue is deliberately active, not passive (like daydreaming). It differs from meditation because, instead of quieting your thoughts, you actively engage with the images, forces, and inner figures/feelings that arise from within. Think of imaginative inner dialogue as active day dreaming in your inner world.

When you have an inner question to ask, set aside 15-20 minutes of undistracted time for this process. There are no exact ways to do active imagination or parts dialogue, but there are various sources that provide guidelines similar to this (Johnson, 1986; Jung, 1969). https://youtu.be/WqlhRLvBkIE

1. Find a quiet, safe space. Turn off distractions, sit or lie comfortably.

2. Do a little sacred ritual to enter the space, such as lighting a candle or some incense.

3. Put yourself in a beautiful, safe inner place that relaxes you. This place should be somewhere that both you and your inner parts feel comfortable sharing. It can be a campfire with seats, a classroom, a beautiful park bench near the water, and so forth. This experience works better if there is a place from

which your inner beloved's messenger can emerge, such as a cave, a body of water, the sky, a tunnel, and the like.

4. Focus your attention. Relax, but stay alert. Let your mind settle toward the question you have. Gently bring up the chosen image or topic that you have. Notice what arises in your mind, whether it is an image, a voice, a feeling, a sensation or even a presence.

5. Engage with what appears. Remember that this is active imagination, not passive daydreaming. For whatever appears, ask a question, or unveil the scenario and ask for guidance. Remember that you are interacting with your unconscious mind, so whatever happens will be like a symbolic story or myth. Let the story develop naturally, without forcing or judging it. You are the neutral observer/participant. It is not for you to judge, but only to participate and learn. You are not the master here. But do not allow yourself to be mastered either.

If some inner part demands to take control of you or makes you fearful, it is perfectly acceptable to either ask for another messenger to appear or just end the session.

6. When you are done, thank your inner beloved and put out the candle or incense. Be sure to express what you experienced through writing, dialogue, painting, drawing, or whatever creative thing you do (no matter the quality). Give form to your experience to help shine a light on this unconscious material and integrate (accept) it as a part of yourself.

7. Reflect on the meaning. Use whatever resources you deem appropriate to interpret what you saw. The inner beloved is less rational than your conscious ego, so interpretation is often necessary. Sometimes you have an immediate insight. Other times you may need to "sit with it" for a while. Just like dreams, active imaginings do not always mean something literal. They are more like an artistic experience: you "feel" the meaning, like a soul journey. The meaning may very well unfold for you in the coming days and weeks like a journey or a process.

Don't rush the process of inner dialogue. Take your time and be patient with whatever arises. Do not get addicted to doing this too much each day. More than 20-30 minutes per day risks unconscious ego inflation (Johnson, 1986). Try to avoid judging or censoring whatever images or experiences come up for you. You need to own them because they are part of you no matter their content. You have the privilege of receiving these messages from your inner beloved. Receive these messages and accept them as sacred gifts (Johnson, 1986; Jung, 1969).

Clients often have a powerful, transformational experience when doing active imaginings. If you do, be sure and do a small but meaningful ritual to "fix" this experience in your mind as an indelible part of you (Johnson, 1986; Jung, 1969).

A Lesson: The Observer/Conductor Dialogue

Here is a three-part inner dialogue that helps you become the calm observer who can make choices about the inner and outer self. This particular dialogue was inspired by Internal Family Systems (IFS), Jungian active imagination, and classical mindfulness/observer meditation techniques (Schwartz, 2021; Johnson, 1986). https://youtu.be/xB3lz56PUcY

1. Find a quiet space. Sit comfortably and close your eyes. Take a few deep breaths to ground yourself. After a few minutes, once you are fully relaxed…
2. Imagine three empty seats in front of you:
    a. Seat 1 is the taskmaster (ego). This voice organizes the outer world, planning, critiquing, and achieving. This voice asks
    How can I get this done?

b. Seat 2 is the inner beloved. This part offers compassion, creativity, intuition, and loving guidance.

Be gentle with yourself. Trust the flow of your ideas. You are enough as you are.

c. Seat 3 is the observer. This is a presence that watches calmly and makes dispassionate choices. It notes what is happening without judgment and decides based on the input of the other two voices.

3. Rotate your attention. Take a moment to mentally "sit" in each seat.

a. Shift to the taskmaster. Think about a current outer challenge or goal. Notice the planning, the judgment, and the analysis. What thoughts arise? How does your body feel?

b. Shift to the inner beloved. Invite your inner guide to speak with tenderness, creativity, or deep wisdom. What support, kindness, or imagination does this voice offer?

c. Shift to the observer. From the conductor's chair, you can watch calmly, reflect upon what has been offered, and make choices. You can choose which voice is most helpful for the current issue. Most issues are outer, but the more difficult problems become, the more likely they will require inner guidance. Do you need wisdom, direction, or perspective? Appreciate your ability to listen deeply and harmonize with these inner voices.

4. Now imagine that you are the conductor. You are the one who chooses which seat to empower in the moment. This is the power of the observer/conductor.

a. When you need to create or nurture something, invite the inner beloved forward and listen.

b. When you are tackling an outer task, let the taskmaster help you organize and execute it.

c. When you simply need calm and clarity, step back into the observer role and participate without controlling. Watch without reacting. Just be.

5. As you practice shifting seats, notice how you can fluidly move between these seats. No part is excluded or silenced. Each part can be called forth intentionally.

6. Open your eyes. Remind yourself that all three seats are available anytime. But you should usually sit in the observer seat, allowing yourself to be guided. This is how to turn your mindfulness into a healthy, self-mastery of intentionality. In doing so, you are integrating the inner and outer forces.

7. After this exercise, you may want to explore methods of accomplishing deeper integration of these essential parts of yourself.

a. You can write in your journal and, perhaps, draw a diagram of the three seats whose voices spoke.

b. During stressful moments, you can pause and ask yourself, "Which voice do I need right now?"

c. You can use the imagery of your inner beloved to find inner wisdom and strength.

This exercise can help you appreciate the two voices you require in order to balance inner wisdom and outer control. Integrating these voices helps you manage stressful situations and fosters creativity and self-understanding.

Using Tips and Tricks for Inner Dialogue

I mentioned earlier that if an inner part tries to "take over" or demands something ridiculous, you should either end the session or ask for some other part who is better behaved (Johnson, 1986).

It is also inadvisable to use living people in your real life as inner figures because this causes damaging *transference*. If your inner messenger is someone you actually know, ask, politely, for your inner part to take another form (Johnson, 1986).

Watch for emotional intensity. When strong or disturbing feelings or images arise, this is a sign that you are reaching a point of transformation. You need to accept the experience and let it heal you. But if you begin to feel completely overwhelmed, stop the process and ground yourself. Go for a walk, talk to a friend, put up a protective symbolic shield, or do something physical to get back into your body. You may need to approach this same issue again later, but perhaps take it a little slower next time (Johnson, 1986; Cwik, 2017).

Do not use active imagination as a substitute for therapy, especially if you have psychosis or other serious mental health problems. Active imagination allows you to commune with and receive messages from your inner beloved. It is not meant to cure your schizophrenia or replace the medication that you dislike taking (Johnson, 1986).

After an inner dialogue, ground yourself back into your body: stretch your body, drink some water, or do whatever routine returns you to a fully conscious state for everyday life (Johnson, 1986).

If you wish to study active imagination or IFS part dialogue further, refer to the References sections throughout this book. My personal preference is Johnson's *Inner Work* (1986).

Active imagination is a deep and rewarding practice that you can do for the rest of your life to integrate your shadow. If you are new to this and feel uncomfortable doing it by yourself, consider either partnering with a willing friend or therapist familiar with inner imagination or IFS parts dialogue. Refer to Appendix C to find other creative ways of dialoguing with your inner beloved.

Active imagination can open doors to creativity, inner healing, and self-understanding. Approach it with curiosity, respect, and care for your own boundaries.

References

American Psychological Association. (2019, October 30). Mindfulness meditation: A research-proven way to reduce stress. https://www.apa.org/topics/mindfulness/meditation

Brach, T. (2012). *Radical acceptance: Embracing your life with the heart of a Buddha*. Bantam.

Cwik, J. C. (2017). The healing power of active imagination on posttraumatic stress disorder: A pilot study. *Journal of Trauma & Dissociation, 18*(4), 473-488. https://doi.org/10.1080/15299732.2017.1366518

Headspace Inc. (2023). *Headspace* [Mobile app]. https://www.headspace.com/app

Johnson, R. A. (1986). *Inner work: Using dreams and active imagination for personal growth*. HarperOne.

Jung, C. G. (1966). *The practice of psychotherapy: Essays on the psychology of the transference and other subjects* (R. F. C. Hull, Trans.). Princeton University Press. (Original work published 1954)

Kabat-Zinn, J. (1994). *Wherever you go, there you are: Mindfulness meditation in everyday life*. Hyperion.

Mayo Clinic. (2023, December 14). Meditation: A simple, fast way to reduce stress. https://www.mayoclinic.org/tests-procedures/meditation/in-depth/meditation/art-20045858

Schwartz, R. C. (2021). *No Bad Parts: Healing Trauma and Restoring Wholeness with the Internal Family Systems Model*. Sounds True.

Tolle, E. (1999). *The power of now: A guide to spiritual enlightenment*. New World Library.

B Using Oracles

Humans have used oracle systems to answer difficult questions for thousands of years. Jung found that some of these systems are very good at "opening up a channel" to the unconscious self. Oracle cards, tarot, I Ching, and even astrology can, if properly used, help deliver messages from your inner beloved (Jung, 1968). Having said all that, some people find this approach too irrational, which is no surprise since the unconscious mind is that way.

When I was younger, I used the I Ching to answer tough questions. But I made the mistake of thinking that oracle systems could predict the future: they cannot. Oracles simply point inwards, toward certain eternal truths that you need to notice. These days, I prefer using self-talk and active imagination because this allows me to talk with my inner beloved, who knows me well, rather than a generic oracle system. For people where inner dialogue doesn't work, oracle systems are easier because they always work. The disadvantage, of course, is that the message you receive will be generic and impersonal because oracle systems exist outside of you. But, when the advice resonates, oracle systems connect to certain thought patterns within you that can provide good advice.

I have more experience with oracle systems. If you want to explore other external systems to contact your inner self, research numerology (Taylor & Harry Houdini Collection, 1926), labyrinths (Büssing, Michalsen & Ostermann, 2023), pendulums (Kisley & Viola, 2017), and color therapy (Birren, 1961), to name a few.

A Lesson: Using the I Ching

The I Ching is what Jung sometimes used, to send and receive messages to his inner self. The I Ching cannot predict the future, but it can connect with certain eternal ideas in the collective unconscious that will bring up thoughts that can sometimes connect strongly and provide guidance.

1. Find a copy of the I Ching that appeals to you. I use this online version: https://www.ichingonline.net/
2. Make your inquiry. If you were asking about the nun dream from earlier, you ask this:

Why am I like a nun in that dream? And what does it mean that I turned into an elephant? Does that mean I have to be wild like my friends? I thought that the bottle of water was like my smaller self, the nun. But now that I am an elephant, I need more water. If I am bigger now, how can I hide from the demon that chased me?

3. Then you throw the coins or cast the yarrow stick six times, possibly using an inner rhythm or song while you do it.
4. Read and interpret the answer that comes back. The I Ching uses ancient numerology theory with 64 universal answers that are archetypal in nature. This is the answer I got when I did this exercise for the nun dream.

Sun/Decrease

"The stoic Mountain drains its excess waters in the Lake below: The Superior Person curbs his anger and sheds his desires.

To be frugal and content is to possess immeasurable wealth within.

Nothing of value could be refused to such a person. Make a portion of each meal a share of your offering."

This suggests curbing your anger and shedding your desires. It mentions being frugal (on the outside) but contains big wealth inside. This will make you valuable to those around you. It recommends sharing your gifts with others.

5. Next, read and interpret the Hexagram Lines: There are three changing (red) lines. The middle changing line prevails. It says:

Once he recognizes and admits to his wound, walls tumble down and others can get through to offer the balm he needs for healing.

This recommends that you admit your faults (to yourself, always inward). This breaks down barriers and provides healing.

6. You need to treat the answer a bit like an online resource, as a sort of impersonal "outer beloved" so to speak, and see if the advice resonates. Ask follow-up questions as needed but try not to spend too much time each day doing this. Keep your inner self balanced with outer needs.

How Alana Uses the I Ching

My friend Alana gave me some great advice on how she does an I Ching reading, and she allowed me to share it here (A. Marie, personal communication, May 2025).

1. Formulate a clear question. Ask something sincere, open-ended, and grounded in the present moment.

2. Cast the hexagram. The three coins method is popular: toss three coins six times. Each toss builds one line of a six-line figure (called a hexagram) from bottom to top.

You can also cast a Yarrow stalk, which is more time-consuming using 50 stalks.

Each line is either solid (yang) or broken (yin), meaning either changing or unchanging.

3. Determine the hexagram according to the documentation and read the interpretation. Each name has a symbolic name, an overall judgement, and an image. If you have changing lines, read those interpretations. Take your time. The language is symbolic, poetic, and often paradoxical. See if some reaction stirs within you and amplify it to understand what it means to you. This is where your inner self responds to the hexagram.

4. Reflect, write or meditate. Do not rush for a literal answer. Let the imagery and metaphors speak to your unconscious. Many people journal their impressions. Free-write from phrases that stand out to you, or create it like dreamwork asking questions like, "What part of me is speaking? What part of me is being spoken to? What wants to emerge or be revealed?"

Using Tarot for Self-Reflection

In a November 2025 *New York Times* article, Makenna Goodman (2025) playfully poked fun at the tarot while pointing out some useful ways to use oracle systems for self-reflection.

People often project their desires onto oracle systems using leading questions that they feel entitled to. The tarot, in particular, is a fun thing that you can use while also investing some personal symbolic meaning into it. For instance, you can embody the tarot with "motherhood" rather than diagnosing yourself with a terrible mother complex.

The tarot makes us all into artists, like children playing a game, as we explore ideas via whimsy. This is actually what I do when using the I Ching. I have a little fun and see what answers I get. But I never consult oracles or my inner beloved without a good reason.

Jung (1960/1952) says we create our inner selves when we play. I've been creating things (music, books) for years, and I truly believe that my inner self has "become" the things that I created, at least in metaphor. I think of my inner work as my "life's work," almost like a personal bible.

The tarot has therapeutic value for believers and skeptics alike, because it uses our agency and appeals to our intuition. Jung (1950) warns people not to use oracle systems for prediction, but mainly for personal reflection. The tarot harnesses our imagination and tempts our inner beloved to guide and show us signs from within. Oracle systems are not a replacement for therapy, but they are a fun activity for self-reflection. You may discover your inner path as you play with this archetypal toy.

A Lesson: Using Tarot

Here is how I use an online Tarot oracle.
https://www.free-tarot-reading.net/free

1 Ask your question and tap on the deck to choose six cards at random.
2 Get your reading.

Card 1: How do you feel about yourself? Empress
Card 2: What you want most right now: High priestess
Card 3: Your fears: The tower
Card 4: What is going for you: Wheel of fortune
Card 5: What is going against you? The Hierophant
Card 6: The likely outcome: Justice

3 Interpretation

This is a time for self-care and in-home comfort that bring happiness. What you want is for a secret to be revealed. You are afraid your whole world is falling apart. Your run of good luck actually has nothing to do with you, so enjoy your good fortune while you can. You are struggling to conform to expectations. In the end, justice will be done: decisions will go in your favor especially with relationships and legal matters.

4 Analysis

Most of this tarot reading is generic, but it follows the troubles of the original nun/elephant/water dream from earlier fairly closely. However, the tarot likes to make predictions of the outer world, which (according to everything I have studied) is not possible. The advice is good, but you cannot expect the predictions to hold true in the real world.

References

Birren, F. (1961). *Color psychology and color therapy: A factual study of the influence of color on human life*. University Books.

Büssing, A., Michalsen, A., & Ostermann, T. (2023). A sense of connectedness, transcendent experiences, and insights during collective labyrinth walking. *Frontiers in Psychology*, 14, Article 1232784. https://doi.org/10.3389/fpsyg.2023.1232784

Goodman, M. (2025, November 30). The fool's guide to major life decisions. *The New York Times*. https://www.nytimes.com/2025/11/30/opinion/tarot-astrology-divination-esoteric.html

Jung, C. G. (1950). *The I Ching or book of changes* (Foreword). In R. Wilhelm & C. F. Baynes (Trans.), *The I Ching or book of changes* (3rd ed., pp. xliii–xlviii). Princeton University Press.

Jung, C. G. (1960). *Synchronicity: An acausal connecting principle*. In The structure and dynamics of the psyche (Vol. 8, pp. 417–519). Princeton University Press. (Original work published 1953).

Jung, C. G. (1968). *The archetypes and the collective unconscious* (R. F. C. Hull, Trans.). In H. Read, M. Fordham, & G. Adler (Eds.), The collected works of C. G. Jung: Vol. 9, Part 1 (pp. 3-41). Princeton University Press. (Original work published 1959).

Kisley, M. A., & Viola, V. (2017). Ask the pendulum: Personality predictors of ideomotor performance. *Frontiers in Psychology*, 8, 567. https://doi.org/10.3389/fpsyg.2017.00567

Taylor, A. Y., & Harry Houdini Collection. (1926). *Numerology made plain: The science of names and numbers and the law of vibration*. Laird & Lee. Retrieved from https://www.loc.gov/item/26014441/

Communing With Your Inner Beloved

Any time you touch the unconscious, you are communicating with nature itself. Open the pathway to your unconscious and become guided by your inner beloved. The list is endless, but these are common ways to touch your unconscious.

- Active imagination exercises
- Art of any kind (creativity made manifest in the physical world), not just commercial art but at any level
- Art therapy and symbolic creation
- Body movement and dance (e.g. hula hoop)
- *Deja vu* and *synchronicity*
- Dream diaries and symbolic/metaphor interpretations
- Free writing/drawing/sculpting or stream of consciousness
- IFS parts dialogue
- Introspection and self-reflection: e.g. journaling of any kind
- Karma
- Meditation and mindfulness
- Miracles
- Music and composition at any level
- Mythology and storytelling (e.g. Women who run with the wolves, etc.)
- Nature immersion (gardening, hiking, walking, etc.)

- Noticing synchronicities and their meaningful coincidental associations
- Oracle systems, such as tarot, I Ching, astrology, etc.
- Play of any kind and humor (projective)
- Receiving "messages" from within
- Ritual and ceremony
- Shadow work
- Shamanic journeying and trance states
- Speaking in tongues
- Therapeutic dialogue
- Universal field of consciousness
- Visions
- Writing lyrics or hearing lyrics with messages

D Using Miscellaneous Lessons

I could easily imagine this section growing to twenty or more useful lessons that I have used with clients. These scripts here simply did not fit in the flow of the earlier sections, but have proven useful and healing. I hope you find them useful in your path to authentic enlightenment.

A Lesson: A Script for Safety and Protection

Relaxation techniques and "sending messages" to the inner beloved are the most common things that my clients do. But when worry and tension turns to anxiety and panic, further measures are necessary. Anyone who is experiencing anxiety or panic attacks should seek professional help.

A while back, one of my clients did too much active imagination visualization, and his anima figure started to "take over," which made him feel overwhelmed. Two other clients of mine were being harassed at work and started having panic attacks. I advised them all to seek professional help. I also developed a protection script, which I recorded and sent to them. All three clients suggested that I include the protection script somewhere in this text. Do not use this script to "bottle up" your fears and hide from them, but simply to set them aside for a while until you are calmer and ready to face them with clarity and compassion.

This protection script works on the theory that you can harness the various parts of your mind consciously to protect yourself. https://youtu.be/SDn8IGmXdnI

1. Find a comfortable, quiet place and sit or lie down. Close your eyes softly and begin taking slow, deep breaths in through your nose and out through your mouth. Breathe in for a count of four, hold for four, and then breathe out slowly for a count of four. With each breath out, release the tension in your body. Do this from head to toe until your entire body is relaxed.

Sometimes, relaxing completely can ease the symptoms of panic and anxiety. This is like an Eye Movement Desensitization and Reprocessing (EMDR) session, where rhythmic breathing provides calming to quiet the nervous system and prepares you for inner work.

2. If you feel comfortable continuing, imagine a warm, gentle light surrounding you. This light from your inner beloved is a soft but strong protective shield against anything that might overwhelm you. This inner shield will keep you safe. Feel the light wrapping around you like a comfortable blanket. This protective light creates a space just for you that helps you feel calm, secure, and cared for.

3. As you breathe in, feel the protective light growing brighter and warmer. As you breathe out, imagine any tension, worry, or stress gently melting away. This leaves you feeling lighter and more at ease.

4. In this safe space, you feel grounded and steady. Imagine roots growing softly from your feet into the earth, anchoring you with calm strength and stability. You feel connected, centered, and supported from within.

5. As you look around, you see two chairs. Invite the part of yourself that sometimes feels overwhelmed or anxious to take a seat. Speak gently to this part:

I see you. Thank you for sharing your feelings. Together, we will stay calm and take care of ourselves.

6. Offer your hand to this anxious part.

Take my hand. We can walk together and I will keep you safe.

7. If difficult feelings arise, imagine parking them temporarily on a shelf inside your protective light. You will deal with them later, when you are calm and focused.

8. Now, with your hand still holding your fearful part, speak to the warm light that is protecting you.

Help keep us safe, inner beloved. We are grateful for your presence. Thank you for watching over us and helping to keep us calm and secure. It is okay to be afraid sometimes. Fear is a part of being human, and we don't have to fight it or hide from it. With you here, we can feel our fear and know that we are safe.

9. In your mind's eye, get up and sit in the remaining chair. This chair belongs to your objective observer. This is the part of your ego that calmly observes and participates in dreams and waking imaginings. When your ego takes on this role, it is like a conductor, calmly orchestrating inner activity. Speak these words to everyone in the room with you:

I give you permission to be imperfect. You are worthy just as you are. This light of protection reminds us that you are whole and loved just as you are, even with all your flaws and fears. You can call upon this protective light whenever you need it. This protective light will always be with you.

10. Now do some affirmations if you want, to reinforce the idea that you are now protected.

I am protected and safe.
I respond with calm and clarity.

I am worthy of kindness from myself and others.
I choose to stay positive and open.
I am grounded, steady, and strong.
Caring for myself helps me to be my best, most authentic self.

11. Take a few more slow, deep breaths, feeling the protective light around you and the calmness within. Slowly bring your awareness back to your body, wiggle your fingers and toes, and open your eyes. You are now protected from within. You can carry this sense of safety and calm with you wherever you go. The next time you start to feel anxious, remember that your inner light is protecting you.

Later, when you are calm and collected, be sure to take those uncomfortable feelings off the imaginary shelf in your protective bubble and deal with them calmly and supportively.

A Lesson: A Dialogue Between Your Thinking and Feeling Parts

You can build an understanding between different parts of yourself that leads to inner cooperation. Understanding plays to the logical type's strength in dialogue and perspective-taking, while gently giving space for the emotional part (Johnson, 1991). Try to use your own inner dialogue.

Thinking part: *I notice there's tension in our chest today. I am not sure what's causing it, but I would like to understand it so we can work together more efficiently.*

Feeling part: *I appreciate you noticing. I am actually feeling pretty anxious after that terrible meeting earlier. I felt criticized, and I am worried about making mistakes.*

Thinking part: *That's good to know. Is there something I can do to help you?*

Feeling part: *It really helps that you even noticed. That means a lot, even if there isn't a solution right now. Maybe we could take a short walk and do some relaxing breathing together?*

Thinking part: *Well, we have another meeting in 15 minutes, but we could take a short walk out by the fountains and maybe meditate. We could check in with each other later and see how we're doing.*

Feeling part: *Perfect. Let's go quickly, before someone catches us in the hallway.*

These kinds of inner conversations allow the logical ego and the emotional parts to work together as allies rather than as adversaries. This helps rational types practice feeling their feelings within a familiar, respectful structure. Your logical side begins to see the value in understanding emotions. It is not always logic, but perceptive feelings that are rewarded by others. A cold, logical person who learns to feel their feelings will start seeming "warmer" to the feelers around them.

A Lesson: Gardening and Being in Nature

I do a lot of walking in nature myself. I walk and talk to my inner beloved. My inner self likes to talk to me while I walk through the park, playing disc golf.

Being in nature means what it says. If you are a gardener, or a hiker, or a lawn maintenance person, you spend time in nature and that is good for you. Humans are a product of nature, and the thoughts they have while being in nature will be whispers from their inner beloved (Jung, 1964).

A great way to be in nature is to tend a garden. My grandmother and three of her daughters are all master gardeners. The following few paragraphs demonstrate how it feels to be with your inner beloved while you are gardening. Notice how there is a less cerebral, more feeling-based tone that is almost lyrical or poetic. The experience is almost like a dream that has come alive with Mother Earth speaking.

Gardening is a gentle hymn to the soul, a quiet return to ancient rhythms that modern life, too often, drowns out. With each seed press'd to the earth, you plant a hope and a promise, surrendering to the slow alchemy of sun, soil and rain. The act of tending to a garden draws you out of anxious thoughts and into the present moment. You feel the earth between your fingers; you smell the scent of green things growing around you, and you hear the subtle symphony of birds singing and wind blowing.

In the garden, stress and sorrow are softened by the patient cycles of nature. The mind, so often tangled up in worry, is soothed by the repetitive rituals of watering, weeding, and watching. In the garden, you witness the transformation of lifelessness into life: tiny shoots break ground, blossoms unfold, and fruit ripens. Each small success of a new life created nurtures the quiet faith of your ability to foster creation.

Gardening connects you to something larger than yourself. We are all products of nature. We are, in fact, the children of the Earth, as Tolkien once wrote. There is an ancient lineage of many hands in the soil as a community of growers. There is a web of life that flourishes with the gardener's care. Even in solitude, you are never alone in your garden. The garden listens, absorbs your worries, and returns beauty and balance in exchange (Jung, 1964).

I think that, above all, gardening teaches patience and acceptance. Not every seed will sprout. Not every flower will bloom. And yet, the cycle continues, inviting you to try again. This sounds a lot like self-therapy and conversing with your inner beloved.

In your green sanctuary, your soul finds rest, resilience and renewal. The garden is a wordless assurance that growth is always possible while still there is life, even after the hardest winter.

Personally, I am rubbish at gardening. I am much better at various kinds of writing. Have fun gardening!

A Lesson: 5-4-3-2-1 Sensory Grounding

1. Let's pause and bring your attention to the present.
Name five things you can see.
Name four things you can feel (touch).
Name three things you can hear.
Name two things you can smell.
Name one thing you can taste.
2. Notice how your body feels.
3. Press your feet firmly into the floor. Notice the sensation.
4. Clench and release your fists a few times.
5. Take three slow, deep breaths, focusing on the feeling of air entering and leaving your body."

Intuitive and rational types, who often feel trapped in their thoughts, can sometimes neglect their bodies and physical reality (Jung, 1968; Myers et al., 1998). They need to engage in activities that anchor their awareness in their senses, such as gardening, cooking, or walking in nature. This makes them feel present and counterbalances the automatic tendency to drift into mental abstraction (Nardi, 2011).

Intuitive types should use checklists to create external structure for themselves. This involves setting reminders, breaking up projects into steps, and celebrating the completion of small, specific parts of a process (Myers et al., 1998). That reminds me, I need to run to get a cup of coffee now that I have finished this subsection.

Embodiment is similar to grounding. Practices, such as yoga, tai chi, or dancing, can reconnect intuitive types to their physical bodies. Doing a self-body scan and some breathwork can help them notice and honor their body sensations, which are often overlooked (Mehling et al., 2009). For an intuitive type, the body is an unconscious part of themselves that they are unaware of. In fact, the body is unconscious for anyone who regularly ignores or dislikes their bodily functions (Jung, 1968).

A Lesson: Body Mindfulness

Here is a mindfulness self-observation inquiry that helps my intuitive and thinking clients connect with their bodies.
https://youtu.be/F8brBxDBvYg

1. Begin by getting comfortable. Feel the seat below you. Take slow, deep breaths and, as you exhale, allow your attention to settle into your body, such as your chest or your nose.
2. Notice how your feet are on the floor. Can you feel the texture of your feet on the floor, where the pressure meets the ground?
3. Now scan upwards. Notice your legs. Are they tense or relaxed? Are they warm or cold? Heavy or light? Tingling or normal?.
4. Gently unclench your hands and let them rest in your lap. Notice any changes.
5. Breathe in through your nose, count to four, and release your breath through your nose. Let the tension in your body go out through your nose as you release it. Do this for each part of your body, starting head to toe until you are very relaxed.

6. Now that you are fully relaxed, return your attention to how your body feels. Take some breaths, in and out, and do an inventory of each part of your body. If it needs to be more relaxed, take some breaths in and out to make that happen.

7. Notice each part of your body. Place your hand on each part and see how it feels. As you stay with these sensations, notice if any images, memories or emotions come up. If they do, just nod to them and return to your body. This exercise is all about being present in your body. Not analyzing it. Just welcoming your body as it is.

8. When you are ready, gently open your eyes. Notice how you feel. Notice how connected you are to each part of your body.

References

Johnson, R. A. (1991). *He: Understanding masculine psychology*. HarperOne.

Jung, C. G. (1964). *Man and his symbols*. Dell Publishing.

Jung, C. G. (1968). *Psychological types* (R. F. C. Hull, Trans.). In H. Read, M. Fordham, & G. Adler (Eds.), *The collected works of C. G. Jung: Vol. 6* (pp. 3-294). Princeton University Press. (Original work published 1921)

Mehling, W. E., Wrubel, J., Daubenmier, J. J., Price, C. J., Kerr, C. E., Silow, T., ... & Stewart, A. (2009). Body awareness: A phenomenological inquiry into the common ground of mind-body therapies. *Philosophy, Ethics, and Humanities in Medicine*, 4(1), 6. https://doi.org/10.1186/1747-5341-4-6

Myers, I. B., McCaulley, M. H., Quenk, N. L., & Hammer, A. L. (1998). *MBTI Manual (A guide to the development and use of the Myers-Briggs Type Indicator)*. Consulting Psychologists Press.

Nardi, D. (2011). *Neuroscience of personality: Brain savvy insights for all types of people*. Radiance House.

Glossary

Certain psychological terms are italicized earlier and defined here. Sometimes, the way I use a certain term is different from the layperson's definition. For example, the term "prayer" is not used in a religious context.

Active Imagination

Engaging the unconscious through conscious confrontation or exposure to the ego and other active forces in the mind using images, fantasies, symbols, etc. This allows the ego to assimilate unconscious content into consciousness through imaginative dialogue and creative expression (Jung, 1935/1954; Ken James & Jung Platform, 2023).

Anima / Animus

The unconscious aspect of a man is his anima, and the unconscious aspect of a woman is her animus. Anima is Latin for soul, and animus is Latin for spirit. While some people are aware of their shadow (personal unconscious), the anima/animus is a "creative bridge" or guide that mediates between a person's ego, shadow, and the rest of their deeper unconscious archetypes. Your inner beloved is a creative bridge or guide.

The unconscious feminine qualities in men (anima) and masculine qualities in women (animus), serve as primary archetypes of the unconscious that mediate communication with the collective unconscious. They shape how people view and relate to the opposite sex and represent the unconscious masculine side in women and feminine side in men (Jung, 1951/1961, 1969e).

Modern analytical psychologists, such as James Hollis, Marion Woodman, Deborah C. Stuart, and Jean Shinoda Bolen, recognize that the classic Jungian stereotypes of feminine and masculine no longer hold true because of social change, especially in Western culture (Bolen, 1984; Hollis, 2008; This Jungian Life, 2019; Woodman, 1990). These ideas do not consider LGBTQ+ variations that were unrecognized in Jung's time (Hopke, 2024). The gendered nuances of anima/animus in modern cultures are beyond the scope of this text.

Archetypes

Archetypes are genetically patterned images or stories that reside in the human collective unconscious and express themselves through behavior. Archetypes reflect common, primordial human experiences and thoughts. Archetypes manifest themselves in myths, dreams, religion, cultural symbols, and other dynamic organizing principles of the psyche (Jung, 1934/1969b).

Box Breathing

Relaxation via a simple breathing technique that involves visualization of a square with four sides. In box breathing, you count to four with inward breaths through the nose and imagine one side of the box, hold for a count of four on the next side of the box, and then breathe out through your mouth on another side of the box (Kabat-Zinn, 1994). Refer to Appendix A for further details.

Cognitive-Behavioral Therapy (CBT)

CBT is a cognitive-behavioral approach of modern, evidence-based therapy that is proven very effective in providing clients with a toolkit of responses to manage symptoms, such as depression, anxiety, and obsession. For example, CBT can be used to challenge the depressed thoughts of someone who thinks they are "a total failure" by listing evidence against this conclusion and replacing these thoughts with more balanced thinking. While CBT manages emotions and physiological components, it often cannot get to the root cause of the client's troubled soul because it primarily focuses on conscious cognitive processes rather than unconscious material (Hollis, 2020).

Collective Unconscious

Jung coined the term collective unconscious to show the inherited unconscious part of the human mind shared by all human beings. The collective unconscious contains archetypes and primordial images and thoughts that are common across all cultures and throughout history. They are separate from personal unconscious material, or specific cultural manifestations of collective ideas, which vary with society, language, and so on (Jung, 1916/1967).

The "hero" myth is arguably the most recognized archetype that manifests in popular culture. Cultural anthropologists study these myths to find parallels between different cultures. Prophetic hero figures, such as Jesus, Moses, and Abraham, are religious manifestations of the hero. Odysseus is a very masculine hero that comes from Greek mythology. His story is more secular; he is constantly on a long, dangerous journey home. Thor, from Norse mythology, is a thunder hero-god that protects humanity by battling chaotic forces. King Arthur is a British archetypal hero-king and leader of holy quests.

Dream Wheel & Spokes Method

A dream interpretation technique where the central theme of the dream is drawn, surrounded by spokes of direct associations and no additional ideas (Johnson, 1986). This method keeps dream interpretation focused.

Ego

Ego is the center of conscious awareness that includes personal identity, thoughts, feelings, and memories. The ego provides continuity of self and, if aware of the inner beloved, negotiates with unconscious forces and instincts. The ego should not be confused with other parts of the mind, such as inner thoughts that provide ideas. Tolle (1999) and Jung (1933/1959) have noted that people do not have their own thoughts. Instead, our thoughts have us. The mind is made of parts that appear to be whole, but this is an illusion (Norretranders, 1991).

Embodiment / Somatic practices

A person is physically embodied in their physical sensations as a lived experience of self. Somatic body awareness allows you to pay attention to what is happening to your body. If you have tight muscles, a fluttering stomach, or uneven breath, being aware of these symptoms helps you understand what you are feeling and leads you towards healing. Physical embodiment is often cultivated through body-oriented practices, such as meditation and yoga that connect mind and body for the purpose of emotional regulation and spiritual healing (Schwartz, 2024).

Individuation or Shadow Integration

Individuation is the lifelong psychological process of integration, described by Jungian psychology, that unites unconscious contents with consciousness to become a whole, unique, and authentic individual. Individuation involves embracing the Self and integrates the personal shadow and other archetypes if possible. Shadow integration is a process that is never complete, perfect, or finished (Jung, 1953/1969c). This text introduces a way to interact with the unconscious through the creative bridge (inner beloved), with individuation as the goal.

Inner Beloved / Guide

A colloquial term derived from Sufism, which emphasizes inner communion with the divine beloved. Everyone has an inner guide, which refers to inner figures or archetypes symbolizing a loving, guiding presence in the psyche (Vaughan-Lee, 2013). This probably corresponds most closely to Jung's anima and animus, which serve as creative bridges between the ego and the deeper archetypes of the collective unconscious.

Inner Child (puer aeternus)

The inner child is a term, often misused in pop psychology, that represents the childlike aspect of the human psyche. The inner child symbolizes vulnerability, creativity, and emotional vulnerability. People often work on their inner child as part of therapy, although it is debatable if the human unconscious is actually childlike. Jung's concept of the inner child (puer aeternus) often reflects unresolved emotional immaturity rather than a literal childish unconscious. Just like the ego evolves, inner parts of the self can go through stages of maturation that begin with rudimentary, naïve aspects, but become more sophisticated as the individuation process moves forward (Firman & Russel, 1994; Jung, 1969e; Rowe, 2009).

Inner Narrative / Inner Mythology

Inner narratives are collective stories and myths that reside in the unconscious mind regardless of the ego's awareness. All humans have inner narrative stories that shape their identities and psychic lives. An inner story is like an inner "mission." People often appear to be driven to fulfill some unconscious psychological task. Inner stories reflect these unconscious patterns, as expressed through dreams, fantasies, intuitions, and cultural motifs (Jung, 1964).

Integration / Shadow Integration

Shadow integration is a key part of the individuation process. Typically, therapy focuses on integrating a client's personal shadow, which is the unconscious aspects of themselves that they deny or reject, rather than the broader, more universal collective Self. During shadow integration, these hidden or disowned parts of the psyche are acknowledged, accepted, and harmonized with the ego, leading to a more authentic and whole personal self (Jung, 1959; Stein, 1998). Johnson (2008) recommends that a therapist should mine the "gold" of the inner self during shadow integration for the positive aspects of the personality that have been inadvertently removed from consciousness during the first part of life.

Internal Family Systems (IFS)

Schwartz's and Sweezy's (2021) therapeutic model, which resides outside of classical Jungian theory, emphasizes multiple sub-personalities or parts within the psyche that interact with the ego and require integration. This is complementary to Jung's and Johnson's description of active imagination (Johnson, 1986; Jung 1954/1969d). IFS parts dialogue fits better with modern neurobiological theories of how the human mind operates with or contains separate parts that work together to create a virtual "whole" personality. This text uses scripts with a mixture of IFS and active imagination.

Tolle (1999) wrote that our ego does not have thoughts so much as our thoughts are imposed upon our ego from various inner parts. Therefore, our thoughts "have us" rather than the other way around. The ego is a mere observer and organizer of unconscious events to aid in our physical survival. Unifying or integrating these different parts is what Jung called individuation. Imaginative parts dialogue is a direct way for people to interact with their inner parts.

Journaling / Self-talk

Writing in a journal or using self-talk often involves witnessing the inner beloved (unconscious guide) speaking to the client directly. These communications are often highly symbolic and may require some interpretation. Internal dialogue originates from the unconscious mind. Most people are unaware of the fact that they are witnessing their unconscious thoughts all day long (Tolle, 1999). Making wise choices based on this voice is the beginning of self-awareness and making wise choices.

Jungian Analytical Psychology

A branch of depth psychology, separate from Freud's and Hillman's, that emphasizes the dynamics of the unconscious, archetypes, collective unconscious, and the process of individuation to achieve psychic wholeness (APA, n.d. ; Jung, 1964).

Labyrinth

The labyrinth is an unconscious "spiral path" that the soul likes to follow. When stuck, the spiral turns into a circle, symbolizing how a person keeps coming back to the same external situation until the issue is transcended or resolved (e.g. being stuck). This is partially based on an ancient myth where Theseus tries to slay the Minotaur while traversing the labyrinth. Images of spiral labyrinths are nearly universal in human cultures, first appearing in cave paintings across the world that date back at least 10,000 years.

Mandala

Jung (1969b) and Campbell (1949) studied these circular maze designs and concluded that mandalas represent the entire Self, including body, ego, and unconscious mind. Mandalas appear in nearly every human culture. They are not merely circles, because they contain intricate mazes within the circle that symbolize the inner path and parts of the human soul.

Magical Other

Hollis (1996) discusses the magical other, which is what lovers project onto one another. It is an image of the eternal beloved (anima/animus), and does not actually exist in physical reality. The magical other is a numinous projection that causes people to see and seek their own souls in each other. This can cause people to bond with an image of their significant other that does not actually exist. Projecting the magical other onto other people is a common source of human suffering.

MBTI (Myers-Briggs Type Indicator)

The Myers-Briggs Type Indicator (MBTI) extends Jung's (1921/1971) early personality type theory. It is used to assess the functional "type" of a client as a thinker, feeler, body-type, or intuitive type, and adapt the care to the type of person they are. The MBTI measures how a person thinks rather than what their personality is, so it is an approximation rather than a precise scientific personality type assessment. No personality indicator can predict an individual's actions, only their preferences towards certain ways of behaving.

Narrative or Storytelling Therapy

Narrative therapy is story-based healing that, when effectively produced, can cause powerful personal transformations. Dr. Estes' *Women Who Run With the Wolves* is an excellent example of narrative therapy.

Numinous

Numinous is an experience that feels charged with ethereal, sacred spirituality that seizes the ego like an external event. This is the impact of an archetype or "divine presence" that changes the conscious attitude and evokes awe, dread, fascination or reverence. Jung (1969a), cultural anthropologists, and others have speculated that this feeling of divine presence caused by unconscious archetypes is why religious devotion appears in cultures around the world.

Objective Observer

Objectivity is the ability to observe or witness your inner experiences and unconscious processes from a reflective, non-identifying perspective. This facilitates self-awareness and psychological growth (Jung, 1954).

Parts Dialogue / Parts Work

See IFS, active imagination and shadow integration.

Persona

A person's ego can put on many personas, or masks, that present to the world as a spouse, a business-person, a parent, and so forth. A person with a very successful persona often loses track of who they actually are because they identify too much with the mask they wear. This often happens, for instance, when a very successful public figure becomes too heavily identified with his/her persona. If a person accepts this persona as real, they are forever wearing a false mask that hides their true nature from everyone, including themselves.

The persona functions as an image that mediates between the individual and society. It is more of an artifice, like a role played by an actor. Shakespeare is well-known for creating characters that are archetypal human personas, such as the king, the fool, the lover, and the warrior. People put on different personas for the purpose of playing different roles in their lives. It is important, for authenticity's sake, to be aware of these roles. A person who forgets to "take off" the role can become too heavily identified with it. When a role becomes problematic, it is best to drop the act and simply be yourself (Jung, 1953).

Prayer

In this text, prayer is thoughts directed toward the inner beloved. People can dialogue with themselves soulfully with prayer to help integrate their shadow. The term "prayer" is not meant in a religious way, but simply as a conversation or dialogue with your divine inner self (Johnson, 1986).

Projections / Withdrawing Projections

Projection is the instinctive ability that human beings have to understand other people's emotions. Without projection there would be no empathy. Negative projections are false ideas that are imposed on others and cause relationship trouble. To withdraw a projection is a matter of recognizing the projection, owning it, and reclaiming it as your own to restore psychic balance (Johnson, 1986; Jung, 1954). Transference and countertransference (defined later) are forms of projection onto the therapist and onto the client, respectively.

Psychic Phenomenon

Synchronicity and other psychic phenomena happen when the unconscious interrupts normal thought processes to "point" to something in the physical world that is highly meaningful to the individual. Synchronicity happens when the inner beloved shows you an important lesson. Jung (1960) calls synchronicity a meaningful coincidence. When a psychic phenomenon happens, it is, essentially, the soul talking to the ego about some important metaphor that appears in the physical world that has symbolic rather than literal meaning. It is usually important to figure out what it means because the soul only speaks when something important is happening. One could say that the soul "calls" to the conscious mind, trying to help the ego notice something important. Many people use psychic phenomena to help them discern their inner path. It is important to investigate such phenomena and not dismiss them as irrelevant. Phenomena, such as synchronicity, can be of the highest importance to people who are soulfully finding their authentic path through life. Granted, these phenomena are irrational, but they are not without powerful, even transformative personal meaning.

Puer aeternus / Eternal Child

The archetypal eternal child resides within the human psyche. People who get stuck as an eternal child pattern never seem to "grow up." This causes problems because people cannot take responsibility or make tough decisions that allow life to mature normally. This often leads to neurotic symptoms. People who hate to "adult" are often captured by the puer aeternus (childish) archetype.

Red book

The "red book" or *Liber Novus,* is a reference to Carl Jung's posthumously published private journal of his encounters with his own inner beloved, Philemon. Nearly everything Jung wrote about later as a depth psychologist was first presented to him in symbolic form by Philemon, his inner beloved.

Ritual / Healing Ritual / Symbolic Ritual

Rituals are simple, powerful symbolic events deliberately designed to take a successful inner interpretation and "fix" it into your memory with personal meaning. Earlier, I described a ritual with my father's class ring and was able to have an inner conversation with him. Johnson (1986) cautions that rituals are inner events and should not directly affect the outer world, such as a job or a relationship.

Self versus self

Personal self is the ego and shadow. The archetypal Self with a capital S is the greater whole of the entire person, symbolized in a mandala, including body, consciousness, and unconsciousness. The ego is unaware of most aspects of the Self (Jung, 1959). Since the Self is unconscious, it cannot be known or understood rationally.

Servant Leadership

Servant leadership is a way of serving your family, organization, your community and humanity at large through giving to others. Servant leadership is a soulful way of serving others.

Shadow / Shadow Complex / Shadow Integration

The shadow represents parts of the personal unconscious that were once conscious but have become unconscious through rejection, fear, or forgetting. Shadow work is a conscious engagement with the disowned aspects of the client that lead to integration and greater self-awareness. Shadow integration is the first step in individuation. Most clients never get past this stage of individuation (Jung, 1953). Robert Johnson (2008) discusses how the shadow contains not just bad things, but inner "gold" that allows the client to grow, transform, and heal.

Soul / Soul Guide / Inner Beloved

The soul, or inner beloved, is a Jungian term for the numinous part of the human psyche that guides and teaches. The soul is often envisioned as a man's anima or a woman's animus, which commonly appears in dreams. They act as a "creative bridge" that brokers communication between the ego (observing dream self), the personal shadow, and the deeper archetypal Self. Most clients and therapists can contact their shadow material with the help of their soul, who acts as a guide (Jung, 1938/1969a). Regardless of what you call this unconscious entity, the message is more important than the one who delivers it (Hillman, 1975).

Spiritual Bypassing

Some people who seek to integrate their ego with their shadow and Self get stuck by avoiding or suppressing psychological wounds and emphasizing meaningless spiritual practices or beliefs that do not actually integrate any emotional or unconscious material. This happens by studying rather than doing and by rationalizing rather than accepting. Bypassing is common when there is fear. Jung (1968a) is famous for saying that most people will do almost anything to avoid actually facing their own soul. Most people are afraid of their own threatening or overwhelming emotions and fears due to some traumatic event (Facer & Mohammed, 2019).

Transcendent Function

When individuation or shadow integration happens, this is what Jung calls the transcendent function. Transcendence is a normal human capacity to move perspective to a higher level. Many logically unsolvable problems are resolved by simply reconciling contradictions and synthesizing a new perspective, which enable psychological transformation and wholeness (Jung, 1954). Most people rarely experience transcendence because it requires a strong ego to face the unconscious tensions and contradictions of the Self. Individuals who seriously engage in self-exploration, psychotherapy, or spiritual work, can transcend their issues through challenging individuation work.

Transference and Countertransference

Transference happens quite commonly when a client starts relating to someone, especially their therapist or partner, as if they were someone else. Old feelings, expectations, and stories are unconsciously projected onto relationships in the present, so that the other person (or inner figure) carries your trauma, hopes, or fears. When a therapist is "holding" the wounds of their client, this is a form of transference. Therapists are trained in how to recognize and handle this situation. It is important during the healing process to help the client recognize the transference, especially if they are leaving the healing relationship.

Countertransference happens when the therapist's dynamic feelings, reactions and responses are transferred or projected onto the client. This clouds the therapist's judgment and can lead to boundary problems or ethical violations. Essentially, the therapist is now working on their own issues instead of their clients' issues. Since it happens unconsciously, countertransference can be difficult to recognize. This is why certified therapists are encouraged and/or required to do internships and have their own therapist to work on their own issues: so they can recognize and cease projecting onto their clients.

Unconscious (personal and collective)

The personal unconscious (shadow) is the reservoir of personal, forgotten and repressed memories. The collective unconscious is a set of universal archetypes that allow for all possible human thoughts and feelings contained in the human genome. The inner beloved (soul) can help you integrate your unconscious parts by gently guiding your ego (Jung, 1968b).

Witnessing (thoughts)

Witnessing in psychology refers to reflective awareness of your own inner experiences, especially thoughts and feelings without attachment or judgment. The objective observer witnesses things. Witnessing gives you psychological distance and insight (Jung, 1954). Being self-aware and able to witness your own thoughts is a fundamental step in becoming whole and healed.

References

APA Dictionary of Psychology. (n.d.). Analytic psychology. https://dictionary.apa.org/analytic-psychology

Bolen, J. S. (1984). *Goddesses in everywoman: Thirteen powerful archetypes in women's lives*. Harper & Row.

Campbell, J. (1949). *The hero with a thousand faces*. Princeton University Press.

Facer, C., & Mohammed, S. (2019). Spiritual bypassing: When spirituality disconnects us. *Psychotherapy Networker*.

Firman, J., & Russel, R. (1994). *The inner child workbook: What to do with your past when it just won't go away*. New York: Wiley.

Hillman, J. (1975). *Re-Visioning Psychology*. Harper & Row.

Hollis, J. (1998). *The Eden Project: In search of the magical other*. Inner City Books.

Hollis, J. (2008). *The middle passage: From misery to meaning in midlife*. Gotham Books.

Hollis, J. (2020, March 28). Soulwork: What makes Jungian analysis different. Psychology Today.+

Hopcke, R. H. (2024). Did Jung understand gay identity? This Jungian Life. https://thisjungianlife.com/robert-hopcke/

James, K. [Ken James]. (2023). Guidelines for active imagination. Jung Platform.

Johnson, R. A. (1986). *Inner work: Using dreams and active imagination for personal growth*. HarperOne.

Johnson, R. A. (2008). *Inner gold: Understanding psychological projection*. Koa Books.

https://jungplatform.com/wp-content/uploads/dlm_uploads/2023/06/PDF-handout-Active-Imagination-2.pdf

Jung, C. G. (1954). *The Tavistock Lectures* (R. F. C. Hull, Trans.). Princeton University Press. (Original work published 1935)

Jung, C. G. (1959). *The relations between the ego and the unconscious. In The collected works of C. G. Jung* (Vol. 7, R. F. C. Hull, Trans.). Princeton University Press. (Original work published 1933)

Jung, C. G. (1960). *Synchronicity: An acausal connecting principle* (R. F. C. Hull, Trans.). Princeton University Press. (Original work published 1952)

Jung, C. G. (1961). *Psychological types* (H. G. Baynes, Trans.). Princeton University Press. (Original work published 1951)

Jung, C. G. (1964). *Man and his symbols*. Doubleday.

Jung, C. G. (1967). The structure of the unconscious. In *Two essays on analytical psychology* (R. F. C. Hull, Trans., Vol. 7, pp. 73-136). Princeton University Press. (Original work published 1916)

Jung, C. G. (1968a). *Psychology and alchemy* (R. F. C. Hull, Trans.). In *Collected Works of C. G. Jung* (Vol. 12, p. 99). Princeton University Press. (Original work published 1944)

Jung, C. G. (1968b). *The archetypes and the collective unconscious* (R. F. C. Hull, Trans.). In H. Read, M. Fordham, & G. Adler (Eds.), The collected works of C. G. Jung: Vol. 9, Part 1 (pp. 3-41). Princeton University Press. (Original work published 1959).

Jung, C. G. (1968c). *The structure and dynamics of the psyche* (R. F. C. Hull, Trans.). In H. Read, M. Fordham, G. Adler, & W. McGuire (Eds.), *The collected works of C. G. Jung (Vol. 8)*. Princeton University Press.

Jung, C. G. (1969a). *Psychology and religion: West and East* (R. F. C. Hull, Trans.). In H. Read, M. Fordham, & G. Adler (Eds.), *The collected works of C. G. Jung* (Vol. 11, 2nd ed.). Princeton University Press. (Original work published 1938)

Jung, C. G. (1969b). *The structure and dynamics of the psyche* (R. F. C. Hull, Trans.). In H. Read, M. Fordham, G. Adler, & W. McGuire (Eds.), *The collected works of C. G. Jung* (Vol. 8). Princeton University Press. (Original work published 1953)

Jung, C. G. (1969c). *The practice of psychotherapy: Essays on the psychology of the transference and other subjects* (R. F. C. Hull, Trans.). In H. Read, M. Fordham, G. Adler, & W. McGuire (Eds.), *The collected works of C. G. Jung (Vol. 16)*. Princeton University Press. (Original work published 1954)

Jung, C. G. (1969). *Two essays on analytical psychology* (R. F. C. Hull, Trans.). Princeton University Press.

Jung, C. G. (1971). *Psychological types* (R. F. C. Hull, Trans.). In H. Read, M. Fordham, G. Adler, & W. McGuire (Eds.), *The collected works of C. G. Jung (Vol. 6)*. Princeton University Press. (Original work published 1921)

Kabat-Zinn, J. (1990). *Full catastrophe living: Using the wisdom of your body and mind to face stress, pain, and illness.* Delacorte.

MentalZon. (2025). Carl Jung's perspective on personal growth without a partner. Retrieved September 2025, from https://mentalzon.com/en/post/4999/carl-jungs-perspective-on-personal-growth-without-a-partner

Norretranders, T. (1998). *The user illusion: Cutting consciousness down to size.* Viking.

Rowe, P. (2009). *The myth of the inner child: Working with the adult psyche.* Routledge.

Schwartz, R. C., & Sweezy, M. (2021). *Internal Family Systems Therapy* (2nd ed.). Guilford Press.

Schwartz, A. (2024, December 29). Embodiment in somatic psychology. Retrieved from https://drarielleschwartz.com/embodiment-in-somatic-psychology-dr-arielle-schwartz/

Stein, M. (1998). *Jung's map of the soul: An introduction*. Open Court.

This Jungian Life. (2019). *Anima & Animus, e19*. In This Jungian Life podcast.

Tolle, E. (1999). *The power of now: A guide to spiritual enlightenment*. New World Library.

Vaughan-Lee, L. (2013). *The bond with the beloved: The inner relationship of the lover and the beloved*. Findhorn Press.

Woodman, M. (1990). *The pregnant woman: A process of psychological awakening*. Shambhala.

About the Author

Scott Smith is a writer, Jungian life coach, and dedicated volunteer with Y-OPAS (YMCA Outreach Programs for Aging Seniors). Since 2019, he has moderated the Carl Jung and the Creative Bridge Facebook group, fostering community and dialogue around Jungian ideas. Scott's diverse career has included roles as an IT professional and executive, a Dale Carnegie Graduate Assistant, a technical writer, and a professional songwriter. He composed the music and lyrics for *The Track Home,* a musical staged in Springfield, Illinois in 2013 at the Hoagland Center for the Arts. He was a crisis hotline volunteer and trainer for the Champaign County Mental Health Center in the mid 1990s. Scott lives in Phoenix, Arizona, with his wife of 35+ years and their two Bengal cats. His inner beloved, Maxwell, was the inspiration behind this book.

www.ingramcontent.com/pod-product-compliance
Lightning Source LLC
LaVergne TN
LVHW022233080526
838199LV00106B/295